GUIDE TO TEACHING A PROBLEM-BASED SCIENCE CURRICULUM

The College of William and Mary
School of Education
Center for Gifted Education
Williamsburg, Virginia 23185

GUIDE TO TEACHING A PROBLEM-BASED SCIENCE CURRICULUM

The College of William and Mary
School of Education
Center for Gifted Education
Williamsburg, Virginia 23185

Center for Gifted Education Staff:
Project Director: Dr. Joyce VanTassel-Baska
Project Managers: Dr. Shelagh A. Gallagher
Dr. Victoria B. Damiani
Project Consultants: Dr. Beverly T. Sher
Linda Neal Boyce
Dana T. Johnson
Dr. Jill Burruss
William R. Orton

funded by the Jacob K. Javits Program,
United States Department of Education

ISBN 0-7872-3328-5

Printed in the United States of America
10 9 8 7 6 5 4 3

CONTENTS

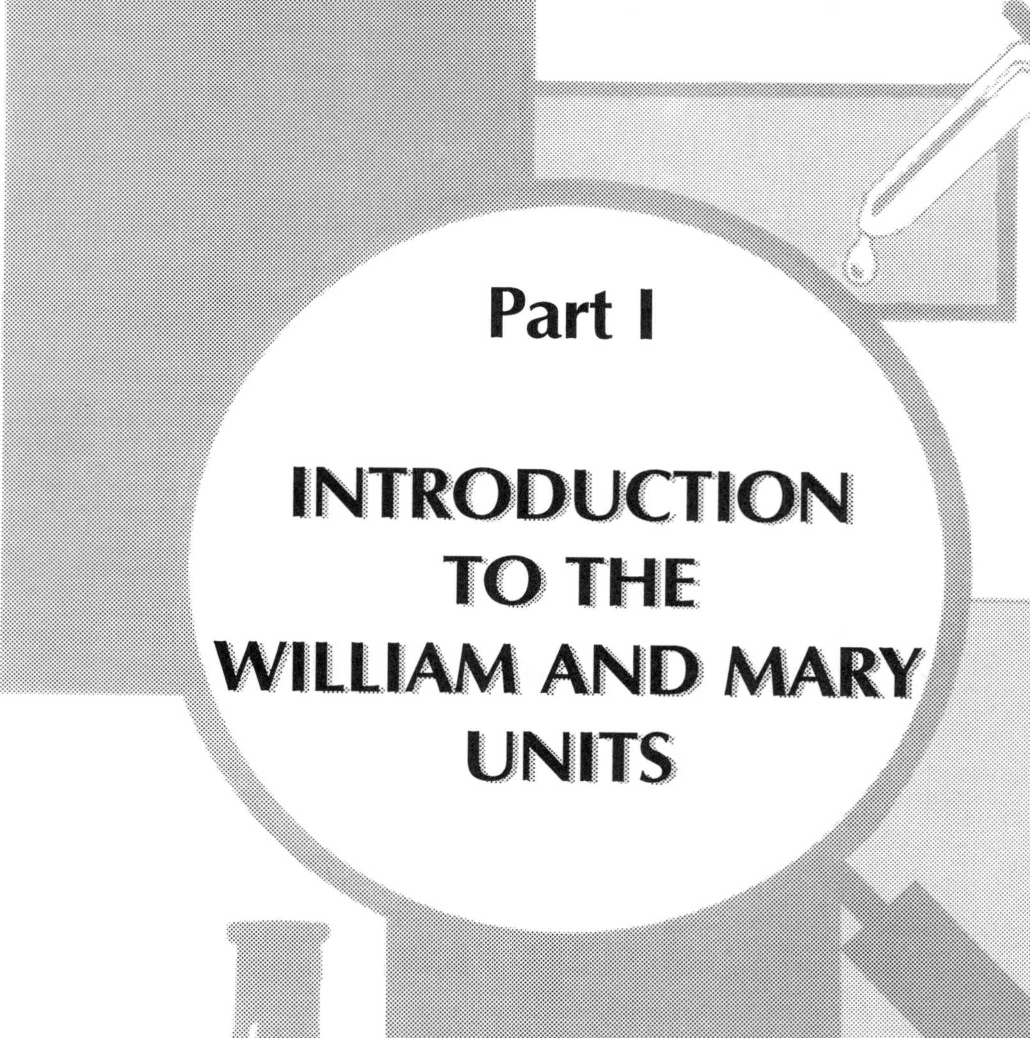

Part I

INTRODUCTION TO THE WILLIAM AND MARY UNITS

WHAT IS THE WILLIAM AND MARY PROBLEM-BASED SCIENCE CURRICULUM?

The William and Mary problem-based science curriculum integrates science process content and the concept of systems through the study of real-world problems. Students learn the elements, boundaries, inputs, and outputs as well as interactions of selected systems. Through a problem-based learning approach, they also learn about how science "systems" interact with real world social, political, and economic systems. The curriculum also engages students in a scientific research process that leads them to create their own experiments and to design their own solutions to each unit's central problem. The units encourage in-depth study of selected content relevant to understanding the central problem of the unit.

HOW DO THE WILLIAM AND MARY UNITS RELATE TO CURRICULUM REFORM?

The William and Mary units were developed using appropriate curriculum dimensions for high ability students but also using design features of curriculum reform. Specifically, the units employ the following emphases:

- Meaning-based: Emphasizing depth over breadth, concepts over facts, and grounded in real world issues and problems that students of today care about or need to know.
- Higher order thinking: Treating thinking skills as integral to all content areas and providing students with opportunities to demonstrate their understanding of them through strategies such as concept mapping, persuasive writing, and designing experiments.
- Intra- and interdisciplinary connections: Using overarching concepts, issues, and themes as the organizers for making connections between areas of study.
- Metacognition: Reflecting on one's own learning processes and consciously planning, monitoring, and assessing learning for efficient and effective use of time and resources.
- Habits of mind: Culminating modes of thinking that resemble those of professionals in various fields with respect to skills, predispositions and attitudes.
- Active learning and problem-solving: Putting students in charge of their own learning—finding out what they know, what they don't know, and what they need to know.
- Technology-relevant: Using various new technologies as tools for the learning process, from doing library research via CD-Rom, to composing at the word processor, to communicating with students across the world by e-mail.
- Learner outcomes of significance: Setting expectations for learning segments at targeted grade levels that reflect the priorities of the new curriculum for being broad-based, conceptual, and relevant to real world application.
- Authentic assessment: Tapping into what students know as a result of meaningful instruction, using approaches like portfolios and performance-based activities.

What are the goals of the curriculum?

The goals of each of the problem-based learning units are:

- To understand the concept of systems.
- To design scientific experiments necessary to solve given problems.
- To study a specific science topic in physical, biological, geological, and/or earth sciences.

How should teachers use the units?

The William and Mary science units were developed to be used as a 30-hour supplementary material to a core science curriculum or as a specialized science program for high ability learners.

Each unit is organized around a real-world problem that is carefully mapped out into specific lessons. To honor the problem-based approach, teachers need to be flexible in both the order of teaching unit lessons as well as the actual number of sessions that students may need in order to work through the problem. What is important is that all lessons are taught in some depth to ensure that the major goals and unit outcomes are sufficiently addressed.

Anatomy of a PBL unit

Each unit contains the following sections for easy reference:

- Curriculum framework: The set of unit goals and outcomes is stated for easy reference.
- Lesson plans: A set of 25 lesson plans is presented, each with considerations for instructional purpose, materials needed, activities, questions, and assessment ideas.
- Assessment: Assessment approaches in the unit include problem logs, experimental design worksheets, lab report forms, and a final assessment measuring all major objectives of the unit.
- References: The set of specific references that are useful for implementing the unit may be found at the end of the unit.

THE PROBLEM-BASED APPROACH

The use of a real world problem as a catalyst for unit learning implies the use of a constructivist approach to science teaching that emphasizes the following features:

- Learner centered: The students begin work on a real world problem in Lesson I that serves as a major motivation and stimulus to their being in charge of learning. They have a stakeholder role in the problem and become drawn in through that mechanism.
- The role of the teacher as coach: Teachers effect a role as questioner and prober of student thoughts and actions in PBL. They exhibit skills in consultation, small group facilitation, and whole group discussion. Teacher questions must provide a scaffold for students in developing an understanding of the problem under study.
- Authentic assessment: Both performance-based and portfolio approaches to assessment are recommended in these units. Moreover, embedded assessments are used in many of the unit lessons.

SCIENCE TEACHING STRATEGIES

In addition to problem-based learning, the units also emphasize the following strategies:

- **Questions:** Questions are organized to address important aspects of unit learning. They focus on understanding systems, on the research process, on the content to be learned, and on the problem under study. Typically, these questions are grouped according to the following designations:

Sample Question Set

Problem-related questions
- *How does new formation change the problem?*
- *What experiments may need to be conducted? Why?*
- *How can we organize to deal with the new questions? What resources should we tap?*

Science and systems questions
- *What should be the boundaries of a creek ecosystem? Why?*
- *What are the interactions between biotic elements in an ecosystem?*

Scientific research
- *How can we test the effects of pH on various liquids?*
- *What side effects might occur by diluting the acid in the spill?*
- *Should we add water? Why or why not?*

- **Discussion:** A major emphasis is recommended on the use of discussion in the science classroom. Thinking is promoted best through discourse, so such conversation is important. Both the student science teams and the whole class need to engage in frequent discussions about their work.
- **Metacognition:** Metacognition is treated in the units through several approaches. The "Need to Know" board functions as a metacognitive tool for students to plan, monitor, and assess their progress on the problem. Moreover, problem logs allow students to reflect on their learned experiences after each lesson.
- **Collaborative learning:** The units encourage students to engage in the real world of science by forming a science team of investigators into their problem. It is recommended that 4–6 students work together to attack the problem and at the end of the unit present their group resolution to classmates, other classes, and preferably to community experts.

GROUPING

It is suggested that teachers group students on collaborative teams based on aptitude, interest, and other variables seen as appropriate. Both group and individual accountability should be kept high throughout the unit. The unit has been piloted in heterogeneous, pull-out, and self contained programs for high ability learners.

USE OF CONVENTIONAL RESOURCES

The use of the PBL units as a supplementary science resource works well with other existing science programs, particularly the following:

- GEMS (Great Explorations in Math and Science)
- STC (Science Technology for Children)
- FOSS (Full Option Science System)
- Insights
- ESS (Elementary School Science)
- CEPUP (Chemical Education Program for Public Understanding)

A sample matrix of William and Mary units and these exemplary science materials follows on page 7, showing the related topical emphasis where appropriate.

Integrating William & Mary PBL Units with Exemplary Modular Curricula by Topic and Grade Level

W&M Unit	GEMS Pre-K–10	STC Grades 1–6	FOSS Grades 1–6	Insights	ESS	CEPUP
Dust Bowl Grades 1–3 (ecosystems)	Oobleck: What do Scientists Do? 4–8	Planet Growth & Development 3 Organisms 1	New Plants Insects Air & Weather 1–2	Living Things K–1 Habitats 2–3 Growing Things 2–3	Growing Seeds K–3	NA
What a Find Grades 2–4 (archaeology/ civilizations)	Investigating Artifacts K–6	Soils 2 Rocks 3 Maps & Models 4	Pebbles, Sand, & Silt 1–2	Reading the Environment 4–5	Mapping 5–7	NA
Acid, Acid Grades 4–6 (acid spills)	Acid Rain 6–10 Cabbages & Chemistry 4–8	Chemical Tests 3 Land & Water 4	Mixtures & Solutions 5–6	NA	Stream Tables 4–9 Water Flow 5–6	The Waste Hierarchy; Investigating Hazardous Materials; Chemical Survey & Solutions & Pollution; Household Chemicals
Electricity City Grades 4–6 (circuits)	The Magic of Electricity 3–6	Electric Circuits 4 Magnets & Motors 6	Magnetism & Electricity 3–4	Circuits & Pathways 4–5	Batteries & Bulbs 4–8	NA
Chesapeake Bay Grades 6–8 (pollution of the Chesapeake Bay)	Mapping Fish Habitats 6–10 Global Warming & the Greenhouse Effect 7–10	Ecosystems 5	Environments 5–6	There is No Away 6	Stream Tables 4–9 Water Flow 5–6	The Waste Hierarchy; Investigating Groundwater
Hot Rods Grades 6–8 (nuclear power)	Chemical Reactions 6–10 Hot Water & Warm Homes from Sunlight 4–8	NA	Solar Energy 5–6	NA	NA	The Waste Hierarchy; Investigating Hazardous Materials; Determining Threshold Limits
No Quick Fix Grades 6–8 (disease and diagnosis)	Fingerprinting 4–8	NA	Food & Nutrition 5–6	NA	NA	Risk Comparison

LOCAL ADAPTATIONS

We encourage teachers to adapt the science units to their local area in respect to geographical maps and local occurrences that bring the problem closer to home as well as through other strategies.

Examples of adaptations of *Acid, Acid* to local area:

We will actually visit a local creek. We are taking advantage of an active historical association site which will photograph and write up our event in their newsletter which reaches 5,000 people in the Lehigh Valley. We have invited the local television station to talk to us about the importance of responsible communication in an emergency situation. We have located several community people who are advocates for the stream and who monitor the stream as volunteers—they will demonstrate their testing. (Revelly Paul, Director, Summer Enrichment Program, Lehigh University, Bethlehem, Pennsylvania)

A field trip to hazmat headquarters at Shawnee Volunteer Fire Company where students interviewed a hazardous waste expert. (Maureen Hall and Sandra Wolf, Frederick County, Virginia)

Since we come from a city, we decided to have the spill at the city zoo. There would have to be a previous accident that caused traffic to be diverted from the interstate onto city streets. The spill would occur just above the zoo and spill into Zoo Creek. Most of the creek is undeveloped and is the habitat for many native Texas species. (Brenda Hillers, Ft. Worth, Texas)

Example of adaptation of *Chesapeake Bay* to local area:

The problem statement for the Chesapeake Bay unit was adapted to the Congaree Swamp in South Carolina: "As a boy, Josh and Julie Miller's grandfather had fond memories of camping in the Congaree Swamp, and fishing in Weston Lake." (Docia Jones, Lexington School District #2, Lexington, South Carolina)

EVALUATING STUDENT PROGRESS

Teachers are encouraged to evaluate student progress through multiple means including performance-based activities, portfolios of student work, and end of unit tests. All of these assessments are contained within the unit.

IMPLEMENTING MULTIPLE UNITS

Many school districts may choose to use more than one of the William and Mary problem-based science units across elementary and middle school years. Based on both the topical focus and the sophistication of the unit, the following sequence chart of use is recommended. Use at multiple grade levels is encouraged to provide multiple applications of the concept of systems, the use of scientific research process, and the experience of problem-based learning.

Early Elementary	**Elementary**	**Middle**
What a Find! Dust Bowl	Acid, Acid Everywhere Electricity City	Chesapeake Bay Hot Rods No Quick Fix

RESEARCH EVIDENCE OF EFFECTIVENESS

In general, curriculum materials for any population have very little evidence of effectiveness behind them. Data on implementation of curriculum is also scanty. In a review of science curriculum materials, for example, evidence for effectiveness was frequently limited to market research data. Developers of nationally funded science curriculum projects often complained that money was available for project development but not for research to evaluate programs. The developers of AIMS cited teacher feedback and positive responses from teacher workshops as evidence of effectiveness of their program. Most of the major publishers of basal texts employed market research and field tests in the process of improving their curricula, but no summative research on effectiveness was done. Lockwood (1992), criticizes the publishing industry's failure to address the issue of instructional effectiveness, noting that people in charge of textbook adoption tend to take the word of the publisher even though they are hardly unbiased providers of information. Apple (1992) notes that market conditions dictate how textbooks are written, marketed, and selected. His work has documented that textbooks control the curriculum for the nation, with an emphasis on teacher-proofing and state testing. Some project developers such as the Biological Sciences Curriculum Study *(Science for Life and Living)* and the Educational Development Center *(Insights)* pointed out that evaluation is in process or is planned but not complete. Other producers such as LEGO TC Logo supplied research conducted by independent researchers who studied the product incidentally or as one part of a larger study.

Although all seven of the William and Mary science units were evaluated, only the student impact results from *Acid, Acid Everywhere*, the prototypical and most widely replicated unit have been reported on at this time. The purpose of this pilot study was to assess student growth on integrated science process skills after using the William and Mary problem-based science unit.

The sample was comprised of 45 classes in 15 school districts in seven states whose teachers had been trained in the use of *Acid, Acid Everywhere* and volunteered to participate in the study. Forty-five experimental and seventeen comparison classrooms at grades 4–6, representing a total of 1,471 students, were identified for purposes of the study.

The instrument used in the study was the "Diet Cola" science process test, developed by Fowler (1990) for use on a pre-post basis. This open-ended test allowed students to demonstrate their ability to design experiments. The scoring of both the pre- and post-test versions of Diet Cola was conducted by project staff after protocol training.

Results of t-tests indicated significant student growth in science process skills between pre- and post-testing for the experimental group ($p<.001$) using the selected unit. Analysis of covariance results showed significant differences between experimental and comparison groups ($F=32.86$; $p<.001$). Effect sizes were high (1.30). There was non-significant growth for the comparison groups. The results from this study document one learning effect of the William and Mary curriculum for high ability learners in the area of integrated science process skills.

The use of high-powered curriculum materials designed with the needs of high ability learners and the new science paradigm in mind appears to result in greater learning on a dimension important to both science educators and educators of high ability learners.

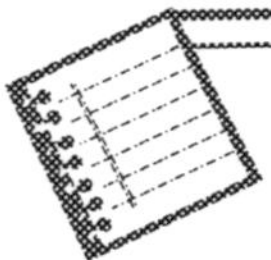

TEACHER EDUCATION

For the past five years, the Center for Gifted Education has offered science curriculum institutes at The College of William and Mary and inservice workshops for teachers and administrators throughout the United States. The science curriculum inservice programs were designed to enable participants to relate local science frameworks to national standards and to the William and Mary science units modeled on these standards, to select appropriate science materials for high ability learners, to employ successful instructional strategies in science teaching such as experimental design and problem-based learning, and to implement one of the CGE problem-based science units. To date, over 3,000 educators throughout the United States and various international sites have participated in the institutes.

In order to ensure that teachers were able to employ problem-based learning with students, institute staff presented them with an ill-structured problem of their own. An example used was:

> *You are a teacher with a cluster group of gifted students, and you are part of a school working to improve science learning and instruction. Your principal is urging you to pilot a problem-based science unit developed by the Center for Gifted Education at The College of William and Mary. You know very little about the units but you have heard phrases such as "ill-structured problem," "teacher as metacognitive coach," "stakeholder," and "independent learning." You are committed to hands-on science but are unsure about this thing called "problem-based learning." The principal's daughter is in your class. How do you respond to your principal?*

Teachers were then asked to complete a "Need to Know" board as an initial step in studying the problem. They were then divided into groups to explore a variety of resources: they could watch a video on PBL, read articles on PBL, or interview an expert on the subject. Debriefing ensued that reinforced the key steps involved in PBL and the importance of accessing different types of resources. The training then moved to the science materials themselves. Using a model unit for illustration, institute staff worked participants through important stages of the PBL process including localizing the problem, locating resources, problem movement, and resolution.

During the institute programs, teachers were encouraged to situate the problems in the units to their local areas. For instance, in the *Acid, Acid Everywhere* unit, teachers were introduced to the problem situated in York County, Virginia, near Williamsburg. They were then provided with maps and other resources about the area as they worked with the problem to design experiments and to resolve the various issues of the problem. Follow-up communication with institute teachers revealed that they perceived a variety of ways to tailor the units for their locale. A teacher in South Carolina, for example, situated the *Chesapeake Bay* unit in her area by investigating a similar problem in the Congaree Swamp; a teacher in Ft. Worth, Texas, used a creek that flows through a local zoo to implement *Acid, Acid Everywhere*; and a teacher near Seattle, Washington, encouraged her students to visit local sites before mapping and building models for *Electricity City*.

Showing teachers how to work through the problem constituted another phase of the training. Sample flow charts on problem movement contained in each unit were employed to track the flow of student progress as they tackled various questions on their "Need to Know" boards. Teachers came to realize that students will learn specific content, do specific experiments, and come to understand systems through prestructured lessons that lead from the initial problem statement. Problem resolution and assessment bring activities of the unit to a close, with teachers gaining insight into what students have been able to master through the self-generated PBL model of learning.

More recently, a PBL course has been offered through the Center for Gifted Education at the College of William and Mary. This course was structured into three strands. The first exposed teachers to PBL as experienced by the learner. Teachers were asked to grapple with an ill-structured problem that dealt with the ecology of a local body of water. The second strand was technological. Teachers were required to communicate with each other and with us through a restricted-access listserv called PBLnet. Because of the dependence of problem-based learning on information resources, we felt that getting teachers online was critical in terms of empowering them. The third strand required teachers to create and pilot a problem-based learning experience in their own classrooms during the course. This allowed teachers to experience PBL from the point of view of the teacher, as well as allowing their students to participate in problem-based learning. At the end of the course, teachers were asked to comment on their experience with PBL in the classroom during a poster session followed by group discussion; they also submitted portfolios detailing their work.

Based on these experiences, we recommend minimally a two-day training session for all teachers using the William and Mary units comprised of these core segments:

- Overview of Science Curriculum Development and Evaluation
- How to Evaluate Science Curriculum Materials
- Problem-Based Learning
- Science Concepts and their Applications
- Experimental Design in the Classroom
- Authentic Assessment in the Science Classroom
- Higher Level Questioning
- Implementing a Specific Unit of Study
- Metacognitive Techniques in the Science Classroom
- Teaching Thinking Through Science Inquiry

Through curriculum development and teacher training efforts, the use of problem-based learning at William and Mary has been employed successfully over the past five years as a way of promoting the learning of high ability and gifted students. It has provided an important catalyst for promoting the synergistic aspects of the new science learning as well as enhancing the elements of curriculum for these learners—one that is interdisciplinary, one that is challenging and engaging, and one that promotes generative work. Moreover, the PBL model functions well as an organizer of teacher training activities since it draws the practitioner deeply into the complex and intricate tasks associated with the PBL classroom context.

References

Apple, M.W. (1991). The culture and commerce of the textbook. In M.W. Apple & L.K. Christian-Smith (Eds.), *The politics of the textbook*, pp. 22–40. NY: Routledge.

Fowler, M. (1990). The diet cola test. *Science Scope, 13* (4), 32–34.

Lockwood, A. (1992). Whose knowledge do we teach? *Focus in Change, 6*, 3–7.

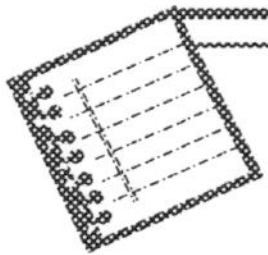

BIBLIOGRAPHY OF PROJECT-RELATED ARTICLES

Boyce, L.N., Johnson, D.T., & VanTassel-Baska, J. (1994). A case study in curriculum review: Science K–8. Williamsburg, VA: Center for Gifted Education.

Boyce, L.N., VanTassel-Baska, J., Burruss, J., Sher, B.T., & Johnson, D.T. (in press). A problem-based curriculum: Parallel learning opportunities for students and teachers. *Journal for the Education of the Gifted.*

Gallagher, S.A., Sher, B.T., Stepien, W.J., Workman, D. (1995). Implementing problem-based learning in science classrooms. *School Science and Mathematics, 95* (3), 136–146.

Johnson, D.T., Boyce, L.N., & VanTassel-Baska, J. (1995). Science curriculum review. *Gifted Child Quarterly, 39* (1), 36–43.

Stepien, W.J., & Gallagher, S.A. (1993). Problem-based learning: As authentic as it gets. *Educational Leadership, 50* (7), 25–28.

VanTassel-Baska, J. (1995). The development of talent through curriculum. *Roeper Review, 18* (2), 98–102.

VanTassel-Baska, J. (1995). Key features of successful science and mathematics educational reform initiatives. *Proceedings from Making it Happen: First in the World of Science and Mathematics Education.* Washington, DC: Executive Office of the President.

VanTassel-Baska, J. (1994). Findings from the National Curriculum Projects in science and language arts. In S. Assouline and N. Colangelo (Eds.), *Talent Development, Proceedings from the Wallace Symposium on Research in Gifted Education* (pp. 1–28). Ames, IA: University of Iowa.

VanTassel-Baska, J. (1994). Development and assessment of integrated curriculum: A worthy challenge. *Quest, 5* (2), 1–6.

VanTassel-Baska, J. (1993). Linking curriculum development of the gifted to school reform and restructuring. *Gifted Child Today, 16* (4), 34–39.

VanTassel-Baska, J. (1993). The development of academic talent. *Journal of the California Association of the Gifted, 23* (4), 14–21.

VanTassel-Baska, J., Bass, G., Ries, R., & Poland, D. (under review). *A national pilot study of science curriculum effectiveness for high ability students.*

VanTassel-Baska, J., Gallagher, S.A., Bailey, J.M., & Sher, B.T. (1993). Science experimentation. *Gifted Child Today, 16* (5), 42–46.

Part II

CURRICULUM FRAMEWORK

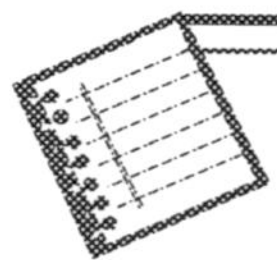

Rationale and Purpose of the Curriculum Framework

The curriculum framework developed for the Center for Gifted Education, College of William and Mary problem-based science units is based on the Integrated Curriculum Model (ICM) that posits the relatively equal importance of teaching to high level content, higher order processes and resultant products, and important concepts and issues. The model represents a merger between the new curriculum reform agenda and key approaches found appropriate for high ability learners (VanTassel-Baska, 1996). The framework serves several important functions, each of which is reviewed briefly below:

1. The curriculum framework provides a scaffolding for the central concept of systems, the scientific research process, and the content of the units.
2. The curriculum framework also provides representative statements of advanced, complex, and sophisticated learner outcomes. It demonstrates how a single set of outcomes for all can be translated appropriately for high ability learners, yet remain applicable to other learners.
3. The curriculum framework provides a way for readers to get a snapshot view of the key emphases of the curriculum in direct relation to each other. The model also provides a way to traverse the elements individually through the continuum of K–8 levels.

Moreover, the framework may be used to implement the William and Mary units and to aid in new curriculum development based on science reform recommendations.

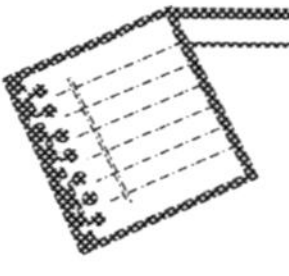

The William and Mary Curriculum Framework and Underlying Units: Relationship to the National Science Education Standards and Project 2061

The general aims and goals listed for both the National Science Standards and Project 2061 are generally consonant with those of the William and Mary curriculum. The goal of science for all implies that science should be presented in an appropriate way to all learners, with attention being paid to different learning styles and sources of motivation; thus, our specialization for high ability learners would be appropriate as these learners have distinct learning styles and needs of their own. The emphasis on teaching not only scientific content but also the nature and process of science parallels our focus on modeling the scientific process; the emphasis on inquiry-based learning and decision-making strategies parallels our emphasis on hands-on experimentation and problem-based learning.

The standards for content are comparable in most cases across all the documents. Fewer topics are treated within the William and Mary units than suggested by the national standards and benchmarks. However, they are useful to a teacher working on one of the individual topics treated.

Generally, the content areas suggested in the William and Mary framework and units are similar to those suggested in both Project 2061 and the national standards document. For example, cell biology and genetics are suggested as appropriate areas of study for the grade 5–8 group in both documents. Our curriculum framework suggests that simple Mendelian genetics could profitably be studied by students in the grade 6–8 group, while the national standards document appears to require a general discussion of the basic ideas of genetics suggesting less depth. In general, the language in both Project 2061 and the standards document is general and permits flexibility in interpretation of the standards.

The emphasis on inquiry in both national documents also parallels the William and Mary framework. We introduce formal experimental design at an earlier age and ask more of younger children. Given the enhanced ability of able learners to handle abstract concepts, this seems appropriate.

The emphasis on applications of science and decision-making in the national documents echoes our project's emphasis on interdisciplinary connections and problem-based learning. The list of decision-making skills of the national standards document in particular parallels a list of steps for resolving an ill-structured real-world problem through problem-based learning. The sample problem is similar to a good problem-based learning problem, and the guidelines for problem selection resemble the guidelines we suggest in our document describing the design of a scientific problem-based learning experience.

One major difference between these national documents and our framework is a lack of emphasis on overarching science concepts in these reports. A second difference between Project 2061 and the national standards and the William and Mary framework is that we do not emphasize the history and philosophy of science.

Tables I and II reflect the direct comparisons of the William and Mary units to both the National Science Standards and Project 2061 benchmarks.

TABLE I
COMPARISON OF NATIONAL SCIENCE STANDARDS TO PROJECT 2061 BENCHMARKS, VIRGINIA STANDARDS OF LEARNING, AND THE WILLIAM AND MARY UNITS

Source	Grade Level Organization	Major Concepts	Content Topics	Scientific Processes
National Science Education Standards	K-4, 5-8, 9-12	Systems, Order, and Organization Evidence, Models, and Explanation Change, Constancy, and Measurement Evolution and Equilibrium Form and Function	Physical Science Life Science Earth and Space Science Technology and Science Science in Personal and Social Perspectives History and Nature of Science	Science as Inquiry: —Abilities necessary to do scientific inquiry —framing questions —designing and conducting investigations —using tools and mathematics to improve investigations —using logic and evidence to revise —recognize and analyze alternatives —communicate and defend findings —Understanding about scientific inquiry: —application of above skills to the world of scientists
Benchmarks	K-2, 3-5, 6-8, 9-12	Systems Models Constancy and Change Scale	Nature of Mathematics Nature of Technology Physical Setting (Universe, earth, processes that shape the earth, structure of matter, energy transformations, motion, forces of nature) Living Environment (Diversity of life, heredity, cells, interdependence of life, flow of matter and energy, evolutions of life) Human Organization (Human identity, human development, basic functions, learning, physical health, mental health) Human Society (Cultural effects on behavior, group behavior, social change, social trade-offs, political and economic systems, social conflict, and global interdependence) Designed World (Agriculture, materials and manufacturing, energy sources and use, communication, information processing, health technology) Historical Perspectives	The Nature of Science: —scientific world view —scientific inquiry —scientific enterprise Habits of Mind: —values and attitudes —computation and estimation —manipulation and observation —communication skills —critical response skills
Virginia Standards of Learning	K-12	No common or overarching themes or concepts	**K-6 Categories** Force, Motion, and Energy Matter Life Processes Living Systems Interrelationships in Earth/Space Systems Earth Patterns, Cycles, and Change Resources Computer/Technology **7-12 Categories** Life Science Physical Science Computer/Technology Earth Science Biology Chemistry Physics	Scientific Investigation, Reasoning, and Logic: —Observing —Classifying —Communicating —Measuring —Predicting —Hypothesizing —Inferring —Defining, controlling, and manipulating variables in experimentation —Designing, constructing, and interpreting models —Interpreting, analyzing, and evaluating data
William and Mary Curriculum Units	2-8	Systems	DUST BOWL—Plant physiology, planetary systems, physical features of weather WHAT A FIND—Goals, tools, and practices of archeology ELECTRICITY CITY—Definitions, properties, flow of electricity, circuit diagrams, scaling ACID, ACID EVERYWHERE—Acid/base chemistry, ecosystem implications HOT RODS—Nuclear energy, radioactivity, shielding properties of materials, waste storage CHESAPEAKE BAY—Agriculture. pollution, ecosystems, life cycles NO QUICK FIX—Virus transmission, immune system, health research	Scientific inquiry through the use of experimental design: —Explore a new scientific area —Identify meaningful questions within that area —Demonstrate good data handling skills —Analyze any experimental data as appropriate —Evaluate results in light of original problem —Make predictions about similar problems —Communicate understanding to others Scientific understanding through problem-based learning

TABLE II
SAMPLE COMPARISON OF SPECIFIC SCIENCE STANDARDS BY CONCEPTS, CONTENT TOPICS, AND SCIENTIFIC PROCESSES

Category of Standard	William and Mary Unit—ACID, ACID EVERYWHERE	National Science Education Standards	Benchmarks
Concepts	Students will be able to: 1. Analyze systems. 2. Use systems language. 3. Analyze systems interactions. 4. Do predictions based on systems thinking. 5. Transfer system concept to new system.	A system is an organized group of related objects or components that form a whole. Systems have boundaries, components, resources flow (input and output), and feedback. The goal of this standard is to think and analyze in terms of systems. Prediction is the use of knowledge to identify and explain observations, or changes, in advance.	Systems: 1. Is something that consists of many parts, the parts usually influence one another. 2. Something may not work as well if a part of it is missing, broken, worn out, mismatched, or misconnected.
Content Topics	Students will be able to: 1. Draw and interpret the pH scale. 2. Identify common acids and bases. 3. Devise safe method for determination of pH of unknown. 4. Neutralize an acid safely. 5. Construct and use a titration curve. 6. Analyze the effect of water dilution on acid. 7. Analyze the effects of acids and bases on living organisms.	Physical Science: 1. Students will develop an understanding of properties of objects and materials. Life Science: 2. Students will develop understandings of organisms and environments. Science in Personal and Social Perspectives: 3. Students will develop understanding of science and technology in local challenges.	Nature of Mathematics: 1. Mathematical ideas can be represented graphically. Technology and Science: 2. Measuring instruments can be used to gather accurate scientific comparisons. Structure of Matter: 3. When a new material is made by combining two or more materials, it has different properties. Interdependence of Life: 4. Changes in an organism's habitat are sometimes beneficial and sometimes harmful.
Scientific Processes	1. Students will be able to design, perform, and report on the results of experiments: —Demonstrate data handling, —Analyze experimental data, —Make predictions to similar problems, and —Communicate understanding to others. 2. Students will be able to identify meaningful scientific problems for investigation.	Students will be able to: 1. Ask a question about objects, organisms, and events in the environment; 2. Plan and conduct a simple investigation; 3. Employ simple equipment and tools to gather data and extend the senses; 4. Use data to construct a reasonable explanation; and 5. Communicate investigations and explanations.	Students should know that: 1. Scientific investigations may take many different forms. 2. Results of similar investigations seldom turn out the same. 3. Scientist's explanations come from observation and thinking. 4. Claims must be backed up with evidence. 5. Clear communication is an essential part of doing science.

THE ELEMENTS OF THE CURRICULUM FRAMEWORK

Based on the review of state guides and relevant materials from Project 2061 and the National Science Teachers Association (NSTA), the following dimensions were judged important to represent in the curriculum framework:

CONCEPT OUTCOMES

The concept of "systems," was selected as the appropriate one to use for unit development based on several factors. In selecting an appropriate concept, the following criteria were systematically employed. The concept should:

- Be broad-based and overarching,
- Allow for valid connections within a subject area,
- Be easy to apply to several subject areas,
- Reveal patterns fundamental to the subject matters under study,
- Disclose fundamental similarities and differences within and across disciplines, and
- Draw the learner deeper into the subject matter, inspiring curiosity and interest.

Additionally, both *Science for All Americans* and *The California Framework* list other significant science concepts for study:

- Systems
- Models
- Constancy
- Patterns of change
- Evolution
- Scale

Integral to understanding this concept were a set of generalizations derived from the concept paper on systems. These generalizations were:

1. Systems have identifiable elements.
2. Systems have definable boundaries.
3. Most systems receive input in the form of material or information from outside their boundaries and generate output to the world outside their boundaries.
4. The interactions of a system's elements with each other and their response to input from outside the system combine to determine the overall nature and behavior of the system.

In making valid generalizations about a concept, the following criteria were considered. The generalizations should:

- Offer important understandings about the concept,
- Explore adequately the scope of the concept under study,
- Be valid for the discipline under study, and
- Apply to other disciplines in a coherent way.

These generalizations were then converted into outcome statements for use at each grade level cluster. The concept outcome statements for elementary and middle school were extended and made more complex in order to represent progressive development in the concept. Moreover, undergirding the notion of concept development in science systems was the idea that at each successive stage of development students would encounter more sophisticated systems. For example, simpler systems, such as small animal communities, were treated at the elementary level, while more complex systems, such as large ecosystems, were treated at higher levels.

Generic concept outcomes

Students will be able to:

- Describe the important elements of the system.
- Delineate the boundaries of the system.
- Describe input into the section.
- Describe output from the system.
- Identify elements, boundaries, input, output (and interactions) as parts of systems.
- Use the terms describing systems to identify the components of the system under study.
- Transfer knowledge about the system studied to other systems.

Content outcomes

For each grade level cluster, specific unit applications to content in science were made. Specifically, there was an example provided in the biological sciences, the physical sciences, and the geological sciences that followed the concept outcome model noted. By providing these applications to the major domains of science, the curriculum framework illustrates how science content may be taught within the broader concepts of science.

The student outcomes in this section are directly related to the systems concept outcomes listed above. For clarity, the relevant systems outcomes are listed in italics after each content outcome. Applications are included for biology, earth science, and physical science at early elementary, elementary, and middle school levels. These content applications are further refined in individual units, tailored to the content being taught.

A. *Early Elementary*

1. *Biological Science*

   Small ecosystem:

   For a small ecosystem (such as a schoolyard, garden, or self-supporting aquarium or terrarium) the student will be able to:

   —Identify the macroscopic organisms present *(elements)*

   —Describe the physical characteristics of the terrain occupied by the ecosystem *(elements, boundaries)*

   —Identify instances of symbiotic interactions (parasitism, mutualism, and commensalism) among the different kinds of organisms in the system *(interactions)*

   —Describe the niches of some of the most interesting organisms present *(elements, interactions)*

   —Comprehend the concept of food chains *(interactions)*

   —Identify the components of some of the food chains in the small ecosystem *(interactions)*

—Describe input into the system (sunlight, rain) and analyze its effects on the system *(input)*

—Describe system output and analyze its effects on the outside world *(output)*

2. *Earth Science*

   Local weather:

   The student will be able to:

   —Identify important elements common to all weather phenomena (wind, water, etc.) *(elements)*

   —Measure important weather variables (temperature, barometric pressure, humidity, windspeed) *(elements)*

   —Record the daily changes in the weather *(elements)*

   —Describe the characteristics of important weather phenomena *(elements, input, output)*

   —Identify the weather phenomena that they measure/observe themselves *(elements, interactions)*

   —Predict future local weather using weather forecast information *(interactions, output)*

   —Analyze large-scale weather trends using weather maps *(interactions, output)*

3. *Physical Science*

   Simple physical/chemical systems:

   For a very simple physical or chemical system, the student will be able to:

   —Describe the physical and chemical components present in the system (for example, a beaker and water) *(elements, boundaries)*

   —Identify important input into the system from the outside world (for example, heat energy from a hot plate) *(input)*

   —Describe the effects on the system of input from the outside world (for example, the water heats up) *(input)*

   —Measure the effects on the system of the input from the outside world (for example, measure the temperature of the water repeatedly as the hot plate heats it; measure the mass of the system before and after heating) *(input)*

   —Describe important system output (for example, the system releases steam upon heating) *(output)*

   —Generalize from their analysis of the system's behavior (for example, they should be able to explain why people put pans of water on the radiator in the winter when the indoor humidity is uncomfortably low) *(impact)*

B. *Elementary*

1. *Biological Science*

   Organ systems and organisms:

   The student will be able to:

   —Understand the functions of the different organ systems that make up the human body *(elements, interactions, input, output, regulation, boundaries)*

   —Compare and contrast the structures and functions of human organ systems with those of other species *(elements, interactions, regulation, input, output, boundaries)*

   —Conduct noninvasive experiments in basic human physiology *(elements, interactions, regulation, input, output)*

   —Create a model of the actions of some of the organ systems (effects of HCl on typical stomach contents, for example) *(elements, interactions, regulation, input, output)*

2. *Earth Science*

The student will be able to:

—Describe the physical characteristics of the planets in our solar system *(elements)*

—Compare and contrast surface conditions for each of the planets and their moons (gravity, temperature, presence of an atmosphere, etc.) *(elements)*

—Relate the present-day characteristics of the major structures in the solar system to what is known of their evolutionary history (for example, the origin of the moon, the formation of asteroid belts, and so on) *(elements, boundaries, interactions)*

—Evaluate the planets and their moons as possible sites for human colonization in the future *(elements, interactions, input, output, regulation)*

3. *Physical Science*

(**Note:** This section may be augmented by LEGO TC Logo work)

Properties of electrical circuits:

The student will be able to:

—Describe the properties of a variety of circuit elements, including small light bulbs, wires, resistors, capacitors, and batteries *(elements)*

—Use the unit systems that describe circuit behavior (amperes for current, volts for electrical potential energy, watts for power) *(elements)*

—Construct circuit diagrams using appropriate symbols for all circuit elements *(elements, boundaries)*

—Use appropriate measuring devices (ammeters and voltmeters) to investigate circuit behavior *(elements, interactions, input, output, regulation)*

—Investigate the effects of alternative arrangements of circuit elements (complete vs. incomplete circuits, arrangement of resistors in series rather than in parallel, and so on) *(elements, interactions, boundaries, regulation, input, output)*

—Describe the structure and function of a simple regulatory circuit (for example, a thermostat) *(elements, interactions, regulation, input, output)*

—Construct simple circuits designed to perform specified functions *(elements, interactions, boundaries, regulation, input, output)*

C. *Middle School*

1. *Biological Science*

Genetics:

The student will be able to:

—Predict the segregation of alleles in a monohybrid cross, using the laws of probability *(elements, interactions)*

—Predict the segregation of alleles of unlinked genes in a dihybrid cross, using the laws of probability *(elements, interactions)*

—Predict the phenotype and genotype distributions in the progeny of a dihybrid cross involving unlinked genes, using the properties of dominant and recessive alleles *(elements, interactions, regulation, output)*

—Describe representative instances of Mendelian inheritance in man (blood type, for example) *(elements, interactions, regulation, output)*

—Analyze a human pedigree to follow the inheritance of a particular human phenotype (for example, the Hapsburg lip) *(elements, interactions, regulation, output)*

—Analyze human pedigrees to predict whether a human Mendelian trait is recessive or dominant *(elements, interactions, regulation, output)*

—Using pedigree analysis, predict whether a human Mendelian trait is sex-linked (hemophilia in the royal houses of Europe) *(elements, interactions, regulation, output)*

INTERDISCIPLINARY APPLICATIONS

Many of the science content applications have interdisciplinary components. Another way to introduce an interdisciplinary focus, however, is to treat systems outside the realm of science in the same way as scientific systems. Some possibilities for grade level clusters are developed below. These applications may be brought in as a part of the teaching of the William and Mary units or treated as unit extensions.

Moreover, applications of the concept to specific content in science and beyond science present another set of criteria for curriculum developers to consider. Applications of the concept should:

- Enrich understanding of the concept and the discipline under study,
- Establish the "connectedness" of ideas across disciplines, and
- Provide a rich variety of experiences.

The student outcomes in this section are directly related to the systems concept outcomes listed above. For clarity, the relevant systems outcomes are listed in italics after each outcome.

A. *Early Elementary*

1. *Social Systems*

   For a small social group of human beings such as a family, the student will be able to:

   —Describe the different roles performed by the different members of the social community *(elements, interactions)*

   —Analyze the interactions between different members of a social community and the contributions that these interactions make to the overall functioning of the community *(elements, interactions)*

   —Analyze the effects of the outside world on the functioning of the small social community *(input)*

   —Analyze the impact of the small social community on the outside world *(output)*

2. *Number Systems*

   For a number system (such as whole numbers taught through sets), the student will be able to:

   —Describe the function of different numbers in the system *(elements)*

   —Analyze the interaction between numbers in the system and the contribution of each to the system *(interactions)*

   —Evaluate the effect of introducing other number combinations into the system *(input)*

   —Evaluate the effects of the number system on other number systems. (What would happen if you changed bases?) *(output)*

B. *Elementary*

1. *Cities as Systems*

   All cities can be thought of as systems whose elements include both the physical structures and systems present (buildings, roads, parks, sewers, electrical and gas lines, and so on) and the human components present (individuals, families, neighborhoods, political control systems, schools, businesses, and so on.)

   The student will be able to:

   —Describe the elements that make up a city *(elements)*

   —Understand the functioning of the city as a whole *(input, output)*

   —Analyze important interactions among the city's elements that keep the city functioning *(elements, interactions, regulation)*

—Demonstrate the importance of input into the city (food, energy, materials, people) *(input)*

—Analyze city output and its varied effects on the outside world (products, information, people, trash, etc.) *(output)*

2. *Language: Codes and Ciphers*

The student will be able to:

—Compare and contrast different ways of constructing codes and ciphers *(elements, interactions)*

—Analyze the built-in advantages and limitations of each code and cipher (for example, which of the systems is the easiest to use? The hardest? How easy would it be to decode each system?) *(input, output)*

—Generate and use their own code or cipher *(elements, interactions, input, output)*

C. *Middle School*

1. *Political Systems*

The student will be able to:

—Describe the elements that make up each of a number of different political systems (U.S., Great Britain, China, the Soviet Union) *(elements)*

—Analyze the important interactions that define the behavior of each system (who wields the power and what can they do with it?) *(interactions)*

—Analyze the effects of input from outside the system on the function of the system (for example, how does the system deal with rioting in the streets and how much is it affected by such input?) *(input)*

—Analyze the effects of the system on the outside world *(output)*

—Compare and contrast the features of the different systems that are relevant for the people governed by them (Do the people have significant input into the decisions of their leaders? How repressive is the society?) *(elements, interactions, regulation, boundaries, input, output)*

2. *Economic Systems*

For a variety of different economic systems (for example, capitalism as practiced in the United States, democratic socialism as practiced in Sweden, command-economy socialism as practiced in the USSR), the student will be able to:

—Describe the important elements of each economic system *(elements)*

—Describe the interactions between system elements that determine the overall behavior of the economy *(interactions)*

—Analyze the interactions of the economy with outside forces *(input)*

—Compare and contrast the ability of the different economic systems to innovate, to provide products and services to the people in each system, and to respond flexibly to internal and external challenges *(elements, interactions, boundaries, regulation, input, output)*

—Analyze the effects that each system has on the world economy as a whole *(output)*

3. *Language as a System*

The English language is a system with important elements (grammar, roots, words) which interact to give the language its overall character and utility.

For the English language, the student will be able to:

—Identify the different parts of speech *(elements)*

—Predict the meaning of previously unknown words embedded in a more understandable context, using their understanding of the rules of grammar and the structure of English words; describe the reasoning behind each prediction *(elements, interactions, regulation)*

—Analyze the origins and uses of words that have recently entered the English language *(input)*

—Analyze how English words have been used in foreign languages *(output)*

Figure I following illustrates the progression of treatment of the concept of "systems" in this curriculum framework.

Figure I
The Path of Concept Development

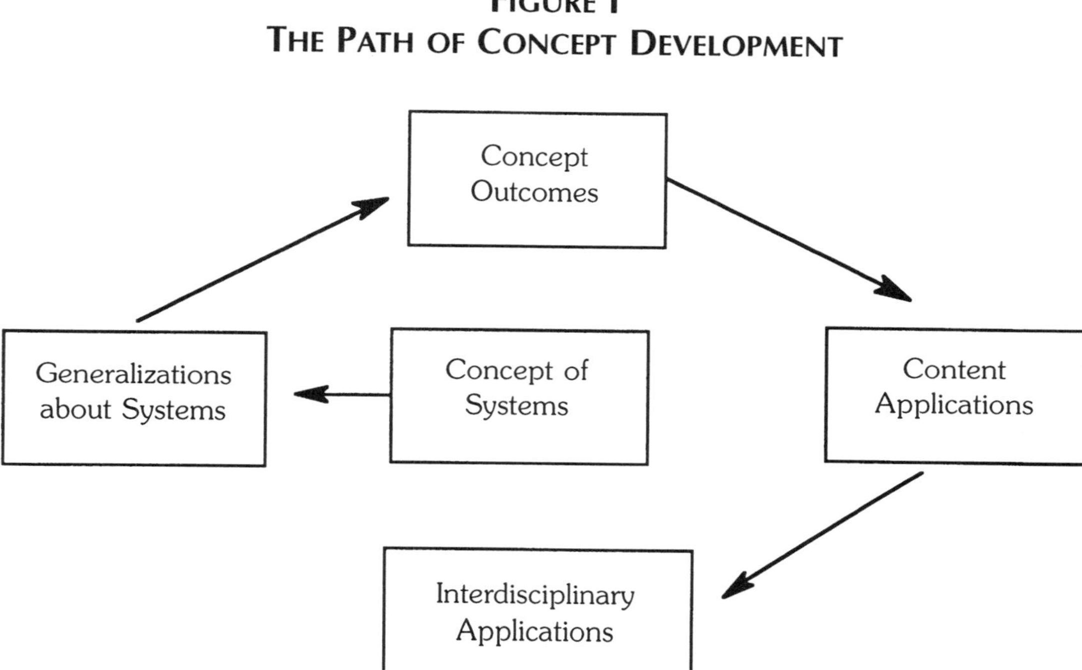

Scientific process outcomes

Also fundamental to the development of this curriculum framework in science was the key element of scientific process. The fundamental steps in the process were defined as:

1. Learn a great deal about your field,
2. Think of a good (interesting, important, and tractable) problem,
3. Decide which experiments/observations/calculations would contribute to a solution of the problem,
4. Perform the experiments/observations/calculations,
5. Decide whether the results really do contribute to a better understanding of the problem, and
6. Communicate your results to as many people as possible.

From these basic steps, the following generic outcomes were generated.

Generic research outcomes

Students will be able to:

- Explore a scientific area.
- Identify a meaningful problem for investigation.
- State a hypothesis.
- Work through a preplanned experiment or demonstration or aid in the development of an experiment.
- Make appropriate observations.
- Create a simple graph or chart. Label diagrams appropriately.
- Record data in appropriate format.
- Analyze experimental data: data tables, graphs.
- Perform appropriate calculations by hand.
- Evaluate experiment results in light of the original problem.
- Make predictions about similar problems.
- Communicate findings to others, using posters, oral communication, brief lab reports.

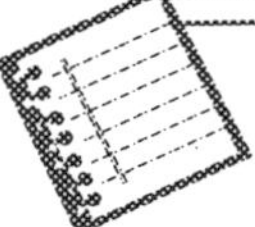

Instructional Emphases

Within the curriculum framework development, the following elements were seen as critical for teachers in their instructional planning. Thus, each set of student outcomes is accompanied by a corresponding set of teacher behaviors necessary to emphasize the desired outcome.

The role of technology

The interrelatedness of science and technology was readily acknowledged in the nature of materials included for the project. Thus the early and consistent use of relevant technology in doing science was emphasized. Particular tools cited for use at K–8 levels were computing tools, word processing tools, data analysis tools, data collection tools, and the light microscope.

Scientific habits of mind

This element of the curriculum framework delineates the attitudes and beliefs of scientists about their work. They closely parallel and complement the major steps in the scientific process but provide an attitudinal perspective on doing science as described by Welch (1986).

Critical/productive thinking skills

Because so many thinking skill models have been used in education, it was important to select a set of critical thinking skills that matched well with the scientific thinking model that is embedded in the scientific process. The model selected can be taught at all levels by varying the complexity of the task demand. Thus students in grade two might predict outcomes for their own experiment on plant growth, while at grade eight they might predict outcomes from an experiment on genetic manipulation.

METACOGNITIVE SKILLS

This component was selected as a culminating instructional emphasis within the curriculum framework because of its important role in students' taking responsibility for their own learning. Metacognitive strategies provide a set of processes that allow students to improve study habits, to engage in more efficient problem-solving, and to provide a process for independent work in science. The fundamental skills of planning, monitoring, and assessing one's work are a critical complementary emphasis to the other elements of teaching and learning science.

These elements then shaped the instructional aspects of the curriculum framework. The elements are presented in a linear fashion even though there are important relationships among them. These relationships were originally perceived to be an interaction of the concept of systems with the scientific process as applied to science content and interdisciplinary content, supported by the instructional strategies of metacognition, scientific habits of mind, use of technology, and critical thinking. Figure II portrays these relationships among curriculum features.

FIGURE II
CURRICULUM FEATURES

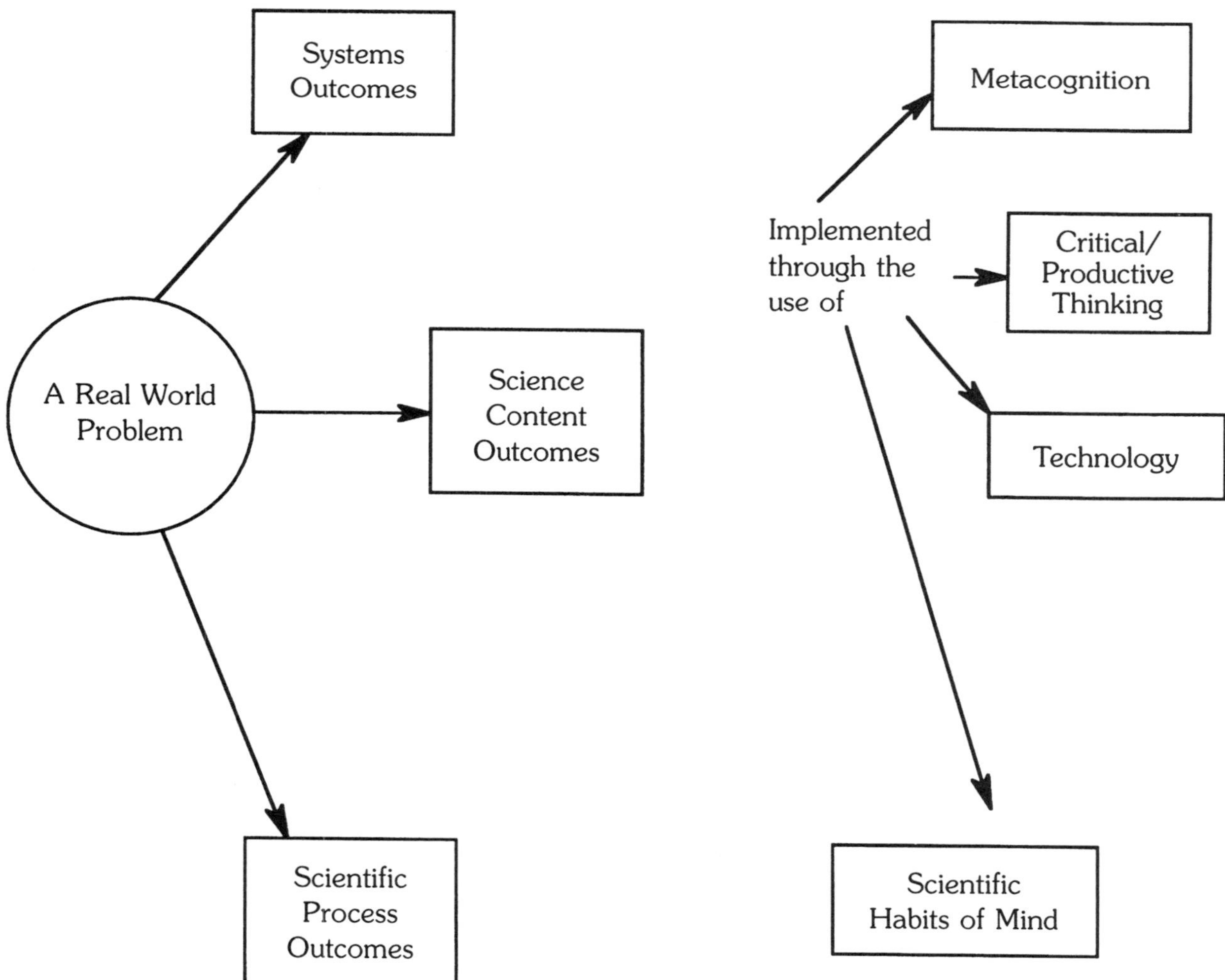

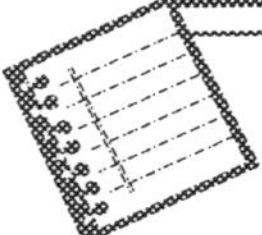

Student and Teacher Instructional Behaviors

This section of the curriculum framework suggests behaviors for students and corresponding behaviors for teachers to use in emphasizing these components in the teaching of science.

Technology

The student will be able to:

- Use a calculator to perform computations too laborious to perform by hand.
- Use a computer to perform calculations too laborious to perform on a calculator.
- Use a simple word processing program to write lab reports.
- Use a simple spreadsheet program to organize and manipulate data.
- Use a simple database program to manipulate reference information for a long written report.
- Use a camera to record information that cannot be preserved otherwise.
- Use a camcorder to record information that cannot adequately be captured by still photography.
- Use a light microscope to observe both wet and dry mounted slides.

The teacher will:

- Provide access to appropriate equipment.
- Teach safety and other procedures for use of the equipment.
- Teach how the technology augments an understanding of science.

Scientific Habits of Mind

Scientific habits of mind represent a combination of cognitive and affective skills and attitudes that need to be fostered throughout the years that students study science.

The student will be able to:

- Demonstrate scientific curiosity and interest in a scientific problem.
- Demonstrate ideational fluency in formulating science problems and solutions.
- Analyze and evaluate scientific arguments.
- Analyze scientific problems from multiple perspectives.
- Formulate critical questions for given presentations of scientific ideas.

Directly corresponding to the desired behaviors for students are a set of behaviors that teachers must use in order to develop scientific habits of mind in students.

Curiosity

The teacher will:

- Provide a wide variety of materials and experiences for the students to try on their own.
- Model curiosity for the students by showing interest and enthusiasm for new ideas and experiences.

Creativity

The teacher will:

- Employ brainstorming techniques.
- Encourage flexible thinking.
- Ask student to elaborate ideas.
- Provide opportunities for open-ended investigation of scientific problems.

Objectivity

The teacher will:

- Aid the students in looking for sources of bias in their thinking processes.
- Require assertions made by students to be supported by appropriate evidence and logical arguments.

Openness to New Ideas

The teacher will:

- Encourage students to look at problems from alternate points of view.
- Welcome divergent ideas.
- Bring information about recent scientific developments into the classroom and encourage students to do the same.

Skepticism

The teacher will:

- Provide evidence supporting scientific statements whenever possible and reasonable: saying X is so and this is how we know.
- Require students to support their assertions with appropriate evidence.
- Provide opportunities for the students to evaluate the arguments of scientists and pseudoscientists.

Critical/productive thinking skills

The following student behaviors correspond closely to the type of thinking used in the scientific process.

The student will be able to:

- Predict outcomes.
- Distinguish between fact and opinion.
- Form hypotheses.
- Weigh evidence.
- Analyze information.
- Synthesize information.

The teacher will:

- Encourage student development of inference and evaluation of argument skills.
- Utilize inductive and deductive reasoning.
- Encourage logical reasoning.

- Encourage syllogistic reasoning.
- Ask students to define problems in a question form.
- Pose interpretive, open-ended, and evaluative questions for students.
- Ask analytic questions.
- Encourage participation of students in discussion.
- Provide opportunities for students to summarize data in various forms.
- Withhold own ideas and conclusions.

Metacognitive Strategies

These strategies provide a model for helping students think about thinking. Suggested emphases for students are followed by corresponding teacher behaviors.

Planning

The student will be able to:

- Outline scientific procedures to be undertaken.
- Order procedures.
- Identify relevant materials to be used.
- State hypothesis of scientific experiments.

The teacher will:

- Provide simulation activities that require student planning.
- Use computer software programs (such as *Where in the World Is Carmen San Diego*) to illustrate importance of planning and ways to plan.
- Employ cooperative learning strategies to promote the organization of small group/individual activities.
- Engage in mutual goal-setting behaviors with students.

Monitoring

The student will be able to:

- Assess progress in conducting experiments.
- Determine obstacles and create alternatives to them.
- Provide solutions to unsuccessful strategies.

The teacher will:

- Provide feedback to students at key points in the process of doing science.
- Help students direct or redirect work as necessary.
- Review students' plans for carrying out tasks.

Assessing

The student will be able to:

- Evaluate conclusions and draw implications.
- Evaluate time and resource management of research.
- Evaluate effectiveness of research designs and process used.

The teacher will:

- Provide self-evaluation checklist for students (e.g., Did I reach my goal? Is my plan reasonable? Did I use time well?)
- Provide opportunities for students to discuss the process of doing science.

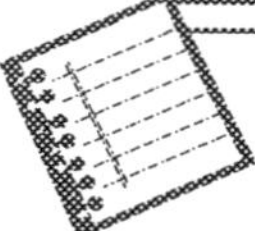

OUTCOMES LINKED TO ASSESSMENT

In each of the problem-based learning units, the generic concept outcomes and scientific process outcomes were translated into specific unit outcomes and assessment indicators provided for each outcome. One example of this final translation process of the model may be seen in the Chesapeake Bay unit (see Figure III).

FIGURE III
CURRICULUM FRAMEWORK FOR SYSTEMS

Components	Grades 6–8	Bay Unit	Assessment
		Identify an ecosystem and its components.	Bay ecosystem web
		Describe systems and their attributes.	Paper ecosystem
Systems: Parts	Analyze the regulatory mechanisms that control the behavior of the system.	Describe the natural regulatory mechanisms in the Bay ecosystem.	Log activity: Systems
	Describe why and how input and output are critical to a system.	Describe the input and output of the Bay ecosystem and their contributions to the system.	Paper ecosystem
	Describe the independent and compound effects of interacting input.	Describe how input combine to form pollutants.	Fertilizer experiment Log reaction to fertilizer problem
Systems: Actions		Describe how pollutants affect the Bay system, especially its output.	Log reaction: algae experiment; fertilizer experiment
	Describe the different types of regulation in the system using appropriate terminology.	Describe the natural and political regulations on the Bay and describe their functions as parts of the system.	Paper ecosystem

Components	Grades 6–8	Bay Unit	Assessment
	Create a system using all components and including appropriate regulating mechanisms.	Write a position paper on regulating Bay pollution and describe the effects this position will have on the Bay ecosystem and other systems.	Position paper; chart of effects
		Describe an ordinance as a system, including all parts.	Log reaction
	Explain the uses and limitations of the system under study.	Describe how government systems help and hinder Bay life.	Log reaction
Systems: Advanced Understanding	Given two potentially interacting systems, identify how the two interact; describe differences in effect of input on the two systems, and describe how the two can work together or in conflict.	Describe the impact of human social systems as they interact with an ecosystem.	Log reaction Log reaction: ethical appeals Analyze the Biotic-Abiotic Elements Interaction Chart
		Describe the interaction of chemical systems within an ecosystem.	
		Work within the framework of systemic interactions to resolve a problem concerning the impact of society on the environment.	Position paper
Research: Exploration	Explore a complex science issue.	Analyze a natural system to determine its relationship with other systems.	Bay web
Research: Problem Finding	Discriminate between central and ancillary problems to research.	Identify research issues associated with problem.	Student-developed experiments
	Break large questions into component questions.	Prioritize the agenda for solving the problem.	In-class decisions about which questions to investigate
Research: Experimentation		Analyze the Bay problem and identify, design and conduct an experiment to clarify issues or test assumptions about the source of pollution.	Algae experiment Water flow experiment Fertilizer experiment

Components	Grades 6–8	Bay Unit	Assessment
	State limitations of the experimental design and results.	State limitations of data they gather about chemical properties and the results derived from the experiment.	Lab reports Log reactions to experiments
	Can name and describe the steps in the experimental process.	Identify the components of an experiment.	Experiment Planning Sheet Lab Report
	Initiate use of safety procedures.	Apply proper safety procedures when working with chemicals (goggles, gloves).	Teacher observation Experiment Planning Sheet
Research: Data Handling	Record descriptive observations about data.	Measure physical and chemical properties of water with accuracy and with proper equipment.	pH experiment data sheet Water ion data sheet
Research: Data Analysis	Create and label a detailed diagram.	Create a diagram of the ecosystem of the Bay.	Paper ecosystem
	Subject data to appropriate statistical tests.	Perform appropriate manipulations with numerical data during experiments.	SAV survey data summary Water ion data summary
	Perform appropriate calculations by hand, calculator, or computer.	Use calculators to calculate averages.	SAV survey data summary; Water ion data summary
Research: Evaluation; Subsequent Predictions	Generate two or more alternative interpretations of the data; defend the more valid interpretation.	Transfer experiment results to application in the context of the problem.	Log reactions to experiments
	Generate questions which are stimulated by the results of the experiments.	Connect the laboratory experiences of pure science to the real world experiences of applied science through the solution of the unit problem.	Transfer of pH testing exploration and pH testing of pond water
Research: Communi-cation	Present results of an experiment in a format similar to scientific meetings.	Present results in appropriate format during final unit activity.	Ordinance reports Bay Fest presentations
	Generate a formal lab report.	Produce a formal lab report based on water sample experiments.	pH lab report Water ion lab report

INTERPRETING THE CURRICULUM FRAMEWORK

Placement of the outcomes at different grade levels was determined based on two factors: the stage at which the skill or idea could be introduced at a developmentally appropriate level for able students and the logical development of a skill sequence. Thus, although the outcome "identify how different intervening variables would change data" is presented at grades 3–5, suggesting that this may be the optimal time for the introduction of this skill, it is not meant to imply that it is the ***only*** time instruction about intervening variables should occur.

Also, placing an outcome at a particular grade level does not mean that all lessons or all science units have to address that outcome, only that the outcome should be mastered by the end of that grade sequence. Not all outcomes can be achieved through all knowledge footprints. So if an outcome for grades K–2 is "label diagrams appropriately," teachers should not feel compelled to include diagrams in every science unit. That would, in fact, fly in the face of the philosophy of this project—that science instruction should emulate real science. Instead, while planning the curriculum, teachers should be sure to include some unit of study or experimental procedure in which the creation of diagrams is a natural outgrowth of the study.

Despite our desire to make science instruction look and feel like "real science," we cannot ignore that school science and the work of practicing scientists are different. Part of the role of schools is to instruct students in the skills which we eventually come to think of as naturally occurring for professional scientists. For that reason, some of the outcomes included may seem a little forced or unnatural. This is especially true about the outcomes in the section "Abstract Understanding About Systems" where the skills are all associated with the ability to describe and operate on the overall concept of systems instead of on the specific application of systems theory to a specific system.

Learner outcomes then provide a basis for assessing student learning at these requisite levels of experience. Students would be assessed in their understanding of the concept of systems in its various applications at the end of grades 2, 5, and 8. Authentic assessment protocols have been displayed for each set of outcomes and constitute the final unit activity in all seven units.

CONCLUSION

Finally, the use of the curriculum framework as a basis for unit development will depend on the needs of a curriculum context and the creativity of a given teacher. The model, however, provides an important scaffold on which to build an infinite number of specific science units. This framework has been developed to provide some key ideas for such development.

REFERENCES

Aldridge, B. (1992). *Scope, sequence, and coordination of secondary school science: The content core*. Washington, DC: The National Science Teachers Association.

California Department of Education (1990). *Science framework for California schools K–12*. Sacramento, CA: California Department of Education.

National Committee on Science Education Standards (1996). *National science education standards*. Washington, DC: National Research Council.

Project 2061, American Association for the Advancement of Science (1993). *Benchmarks for science literacy*. NY: Oxford University Press.

Rutherford, F. J., & Ahlgren, A. (1989). *Science for all Americans*. NY: Oxford University Press.

Welch, W. (1986). A research-based approach to science learning. In D. Holdzkom and P. Lutz (Eds.). *Research within reach: Science education*. Washington, DC: National Science Teachers Association.

Part III

IMPLEMENTATION ISSUES

SCIENCE CONCEPTS CENTRAL TO IMPLEMENTATION OF THE WILLIAM AND MARY UNITS

The following two concept papers describe broad, overarching, scientifically grounded concepts common to many branches of science. They were chosen with reference to the concepts selected by Rutherford and Ahlgren in *Science for All Americans* (1990), those selected by the writers of the California Framework, and those selected by Horace F. Judson for his book *Search for Solutions* (1980). Additional criteria applied to selecting the concepts in this project were: 1) ease of applicability to all science areas, 2) numerous valid connections to non-science domains of inquiry, and 3) nature of being highly workable to demonstrate content manifestations at the unit level of analysis.

Each of the concept papers defines the concept in question; gives examples of its relevance to a number of areas of inquiry, both scientific and nonscientific; gives a rationale for teaching the concept; and lists suggestions for teaching the concept to high ability learners at different grade levels. References and additional readings for each concept are cited in the bibliography at the end of each paper.

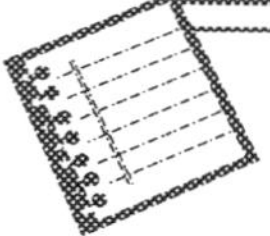

THE CONCEPT OF SYSTEMS

A system is a collection of things and processes that interact with each other and together constitute a meaningful whole. Examples from the realm of science include atoms, chemical reaction systems, individual cells, organs, organ systems, organisms, ecosystems, solar systems, and galaxies; nonscience examples include sewer systems, political systems, the banking system, transportation systems, and so on. All systems share certain properties. These include:

1. Systems have identifiable elements.
2. Systems have definable boundaries.
3. Most systems receive input in the form of material or information from outside their boundaries and generate output to the world outside their boundaries.
4. The interactions of a system's elements with each other and their response to input from outside the system combine to determine the overall nature and behavior of the system.

Systems are made up of identifiable elements and processes. The elements comprising an ecosystem, for example, include all of the organisms present as well as all of the physical features of the area that the ecosystem occupies. The elements of a forest ecosystem would include the different trees, bushes, and smaller plants; the insects, birds, and other animals present; the nature of the terrain; the quality of the soil; the availability of water; the weather; and so on. Defining the elements of an ecosystem thoroughly is a large task. Similarly, the elements of nonscience systems are clearly definable. A school system would include all of the physical property appertaining to the schools and their administration: schools, playgrounds, buses, administration buildings, and so on. It also includes all of the teachers, pupils, administrators, and (ideally) parents.

The boundaries of systems must also be defined. The boundaries of an ecosystem are defined physically: they are the boundaries of the territory that it occcupies. Thus, the boundary of a forest ecosystem is the edge of the forest. An ecosystem's boundaries can be drawn somewhat arbitrarily; one can speak of a backyard ecosystem or of the planetary ecosystem. The first ecosystem would thus be an element of the second ecosystem. The appropriate choice of boundaries for an ecosystem depends on the phenomena that one wishes to study: to study global warming, it is necessary to include the whole planet, but a study of the effects of man on the alpine tundra could involve only a single mountaintop. Similarly, the boundaries of nonscience systems can be defined in somewhat arbitrary ways, depending on the nature of the process under study. The boundaries of a school system could be chosen to exclude neighboring systems and the Federal Government: although all of these elements can affect the school system, they are not really integral to its behavior.

Drawing the boundaries of a system appropriately can reveal much about its nature and behavior. Including phenomena and elements that are irrelevant to the properties under study will make understanding the system unnecessarily difficult. Including detailed consideration of the daily actions of members of the Williamsburg City Council in a study of the overall behavior of the American political system adds variables that are probably insignificant for the behavior of the system as a whole and therefore makes the study of the system unnecessarily difficult. Excluding the press from the system, however, probably decreases the understanding of the system, even though the press is not a formally defined branch of government. Although the press could be considered as an external factor that produces input into the system, in practice the actions of the press are so tightly intermeshed with the actions of those that run the government that excluding the press from the government system would make understanding the system more difficult rather than less.

As discussed in *Science For All Americans* (1990), one of the best examples of the importance of properly defining the boundaries and elements of an experimental system is Louis Pasteur's elegant experimental solution for the problem of the spontaneous generation of living organisms. Before the nineteenth century, it was widely believed that living organisms arose spontaneously from nonliving matter, without benefit of the action of other living things. Rats and mice were thought to arise spontaneously from old rags; maggots from old meat. In the 1800s, Louis Pasteur approached this problem experimentally and resolved it. He showed that if flies were kept from contact with meat, no maggots subsequently arose from it; and if meat broth was boiled and then kept in sealed flasks or in flasks that allowed the entry of air but not of dust particles, then the broth did not spoil. By drawing the boundaries of his experimental system to exclude certain elements (namely flies and bacteria), Pasteur proved that meat alone was insufficient to generate maggots and meat broth alone did not spoil. Thus, the doctrine of spontaneous generation was laid to rest.

Another example of the importance of correctly understanding of the boundaries and elements integral to a system comes from the controversy over the origin of life on Earth. The science of thermodynamics has been used (inappropriately) to argue that life could not have evolved from nonliving chemicals through simple life forms and up to the many complex forms that we see today; this argument is based on a misunderstanding of the boundaries of the system in which life evolved and an incomplete understanding of thermodynamics. Thermodynamics is the science that sets the limits on the energy efficiency and possible outcome of physical and chemical processes. The three laws of thermodynamics can be summarized as follows:

1. Energy can neither be created nor destroyed, only transferred or changed from one form to another.
2. In an irreversible process, the entropy (degree of disorder) of the universe increases; only in a reversible process will it stay constant. The entropy of the universe cannot decrease.
3. At the temperature absolute zero, the entropy of perfect crystals and compounds is zero.

The second law of thermodynamics has been misused to argue that life could not possibly have evolved, because over time the complexity of living things has increased, and hence the system of life on Earth has become more ordered, not more disordered. The basic flaw in this argument is that its proponents have neglected to include the sun in their calculations. Solar energy is the source of most of the energy used by organisms; thus the thermodynamic properties of the sun must be included in the system. The net entropy of the sun has increased by a degree that is orders of magnitude greater than the degree of entropy decrease caused by the origin and actions of all life on Earth; thus, the entropy of the universe has increased, as it theoretically should.

A third fundamental property of systems is that they can receive input from and act on the world outside their boundaries. Input into a school system, for example, includes Federal financial and material assistance. Output from a school system includes educated students. Input into an ecosystem includes such things as solar energy; output from an ecosystem includes such things as carbon dioxide released into the atmosphere as a result of animal respiration and oxygen released by plants.

The final fundamental property of a system is that its overall behavior depends on the properties and interactions of its parts. For example, understanding the behavior of an ecosystem (for example, whether it is stable or likely to change, whether it is delicate and sensitive to the incursions of man or whether it can survive human influence with few changes) depends upon understanding the roles of the different elements in the ecosystem and their interactions. Thus, prediction of the number of deer that can be safely hunted in a given area depends upon knowing how fast they reproduce, which wild predators are present and what percentage of the deer population they kill, whether disease is present in the deer population and likely to reduce numbers substantially, which plants the deer use for food and how many deer the plant population can support without being reduced too far to replace itself, and so on.

This dependence of the behavior of the whole system on the properties and interactions of its parts is also seen in nonscience systems. The behavior of the Federal Government depends on the actions and motivations of its members, their interactions with each other, and their reactions to input from their constituents and from the outside world. The behavior of the local sewer system depends on the amount of material it receives, the age of the pipes, the capacity of the treatment plant, and so on. Attempting to understand the behavior of the whole system based on the nature of its parts is the essence of the philosophy of reductionism, which has been a highly successful approach to the study of systems in general.

Rationale for Teaching the Concept

The understanding of the behavior of one system will help understanding of other systems. Defining the elements, boundaries, inputs and outputs of a system helps to understand its behavior as a whole. Once a child has learned to do this for a simple system, he will be able to apply the process to other, more complex systems. This will help him understand the scientific process, as setting up successful experiments involves determining which elements should be included and paying close attention to the inputs and outputs of the system; varying the elements present in the experimental system may well change the experimental outcome in ways that illuminate the functioning of the system. More generally, the study of certain scientific systems will deepen a child's understanding of the world around him. Every child should have some understanding of the ecosystem of which he is an element and the solar system in which he resides.

SUGGESTED APPLICATIONS

There are two different ways to approach the concept of systems with children. The first involves weaving it into the experimental work that they do in the course of their science studies. Defining the experimental system thoroughly and paying attention to the essential variables in the system and excluding the others from consideration are activities critical to any lab science course. The second approach to the concept involves teaching them about some basic scientific systems. Many scientific systems are accessible to children, at least at a simple level. These include systems from many disciplines, including chemistry, geology, biology, and astronomy, as listed (albeit in incomplete fashion) following:

Biology
ecosystems
organ systems
organisms: physiology, behavior

Chemistry
chemical reaction systems

Geology
the planet Earth as a geological system: plate tectonics and its manifestations
geologic change in mountain ranges, river systems, and the like

Meteorology
weather systems

Astronomy
solar systems
galaxies
Earth-moon system

PROBLEM-BASED LEARNING

The following is an example of a problem-based learning situation that could be used to illustrate the system concept.

The Problem: You own a gardening store. Several townspeople have signed a petition asking you to stop selling some of your products. What should you do?

Areas for students to explore:

1. The garden as a system: look at the interactions of the plants and animals present and seek to minimize animal and disease destruction of the plants.
2. Organic farming techniques
3. Resistant plant varieties
4. Plant varieties that are suitable for the local area's soil conditions, sun-shade conditions, and weather patterns.

Activities for students:

Plant and tend two gardens: an organic garden and a garden in which chemical fertilizers, insecticides, and herbicides are used. Record the amount and kinds of work needed to maintain each; the amounts of chemicals used in the chemical garden; and the yields of the different fruits, vegetables, and flowers planted in each. Report results.

References

Judson, H.F. (1980). *The search for solutions.* NY: Holt, Rinehart, & Winston.

Rutherford, F.J., & Ahlgren, A. (1989). *Science for all Americans.* NY: Oxford University Press.

The Nature of Scientific Process

What is science? Science is a process, a mode of inquiry about the world that surrounds us. Although different scientific disciplines are concerned with different facets of the natural world, they share some common approaches and characteristics. Scientists will deny that there is any special "scientific method," but in fact there are many similarities in the ways that scientists from different fields approach problems and in the standards that they set for scientific work. This concept paper will first explore the research process and then discuss the standards that distinguish "good" science from "bad" science and pseudoscience.

The Research Process

The research process is very similar across all scientific disciplines. This process contains elements of the "scientific method," although it is more complicated and less clear-cut than the standard litany of steps would suggest. The usual description of the scientific method consists of the following steps:

1. Generate a hypothesis.
2. Test the hypothesis experimentally.
3. Based on an analysis of the results of the experiment, reach a logical conclusion.

A more accurate description of the scientific research process includes the following steps:

1. Learn a great deal about your field.
2. Think of a good (interesting, important, and tractable) problem.
3. Decide which experiments/observations/calculations would contribute to a solution of the problem.
4. Perform the experiments/observations/calculations.
5. Decide whether the results really do contribute to a better understanding of the problem. If they don't, return to either step 2 (if you're very discouraged) or step 3. If they do, go to step 6.
6. Communicate your results to as many people as possible. If they're patentable, tell your lawyer before you tell anyone else, and write a patent application or two. Publish them in a scientific journal (or *The New York Times*); go to conferences and talk about them; tell all of your friends.

For the purposes of teaching science, the most important of the steps outlined above are probably steps 1–3 and step 6. These will now be discussed in detail.

Steps 1–3 should really be discussed together, as they are the most intellectually challenging part of the scientific process. The first step seems very obvious, yet is very important. The cutting edge of research is a long way from the level of the novice in most fields of science. In order to know approximately where the cutting edge of their discipline lies and to be able to adequately comprehend the latest research papers, most people must have at least an undergraduate degree in their discipline and some additional postgraduate courses. The body of available information is very large in essentially every area of science; in addition, some specialties (such as high energy physics) also require a great deal of math, some of which is taught at the graduate level. Without an understanding of the math necessary for the discipline and a knowledge of at least the general shape of the field, the identification of a good problem is very difficult and its efficient solution is unlikely. In fact, the graduate education process is really an apprenticeship in finding and solving scientific problems; a Ph.D. degree is the union card that promises that a person should be competent to do original science. The acquisition of scientific knowledge must not stop after graduate courses end, either. Scientists spend a large amount of time sitting in seminars in which other people discuss their latest work, reading journals, and discussing the latest scientific gossip with their colleagues. One of the most exciting things about being a scientist is that the field changes every day, so there's always something new to think about.

The next step in the process is the identification of a good problem. A good scientific problem has a number of characteristics. First, the problem should be interesting to the scientific community and have some inherent importance. These two characteristics will be obvious to the person who thinks of the problem (providing, of course, that he has fulfilled step 1 adequately) and to his colleagues; they might not be obvious to a novice or the lay public. Second (and here begins step 3), the problem must be amenable to solution. If the problem is experimentally untestable or if the experiments required to solve it are technically almost impossible, incredibly expensive, or require several lifetimes to complete, then the problem should be shelved until new approaches become available.

After the problem has been identified and an experimental approach to its resolution has been outlined, the experiments/observations/calculations can be performed and the results recorded. The results are analyzed and the scientist determines whether they are a significant contribution to the understanding of the original scientific problem. At this stage, the original statement of the problem may be refined and more work may be performed if necessary. Once the scientist is satisfied that her work is ready for sharing (see step 5), the results are communicated to the rest of the scientific community.

Because of the reward system in science, communication usually occurs as rapidly as possible. Scientific priority is determined by who publishes an idea first; great scientific races occur in which competing laboratories rush to publish their results before their competitors can do likewise. Although this is not always beneficial (incomplete information and incorrect results occasionally get published as a result of such competitions), the incentive to publish quickly does speed the progress of science. Once the information is generally available, it becomes part of the education process for other scientists and the cycle begins anew.

New information, even new information published in reputable journals, is not automatically accepted, however. It is first subjected to the critical evaluation of the scientific community. This evaluation process usually begins informally, when scientists discuss their newest results with their coworkers. More formal evaluation comes during the process of peer review, which is required for publication in most reputable journals: a panel of anonymous reviewers who are all scientists working in the same area as the authors of the submitted paper must approve the publication of the paper before it is accepted for publication by the journal. Finally, every scientist who reads the journal article carefully subjects it to the same critical evaluation process.

The standards by which new scientific information is judged are remarkably constant across scientific discipline lines. These standards are learned by experience, both experience in reading the literature and experience doing science. Some of their general features are discussed in the next section.

SCIENTIFIC STANDARDS: GOOD SCIENCE, BAD SCIENCE, AND PSEUDOSCIENCE

When evaluating a new piece of scientific information, a scientist will try to consider both the implications of the information and the way in which it was obtained. Much of this should be available in the research paper that formally presents the new information. Research papers from many different scientific disciplines share a common format designed to make the reading and review of these papers as efficient as possible. The sections are usually arranged as follows:

1. Title.
2. Authors' names and institutional affiliations.
3. Abstract: a one-paragraph summary of the work.
4. Introduction: a short explanation of the scientific context of the work; a rationale for exploration of the scientific problem.
5. Materials and Methods: A list of the sources of all experimental materials and a description of the experimental methods employed.
6. Results: A description of the results of the experiments/observations/calculations; should be acccompanied by as much of the raw data as is practical to present, along with summary tables and figures.
7. Discussion/Conclusions: A description of the implications of the results; often contains speculative material.
8. References: A list of the publications cited in the text, along with attribution for unpublished material; every scientific assertion that is not either based on general knowledge or based on the experimental results discussed in the paper must have a reference to back it up. Isaac Newton need not be cited for his gravitational theories, but unpublished data from a colleague or recently published data from a competitor must be cited appropriately.

So, what features distinguish good science from bad science? Some features can be found in the research paper itself. Are the calculations correct? Have appropriate statistical methods been used in the data analysis? Are the results statistically significant, and if so, by how many standard deviations? Are the assertions made in the discussion consistent with the data presented in the paper? Is the series of experiments/calculations/observations described sufficient to solve the problem unequivocally, or are there logical flaws or omissions that would lead to the possibility of other interpretations of the data? Were adequate control experiments performed? Were the experiments performed in such a way as to exclude investigator bias (for example, the use of double blind methods in medical experiments)? Is there sufficient detail in the methods section that a scientist versed in the methods described would have a reasonable chance of being able to repeat the experiments/observations/calculations? Is the quality of the data shown high, or does it look as though the data weren't very clean? Are the results interesting, or did the authors spend a lot of time working on a problem that nobody else cares about or ever will care about? Different scientists reading the same research paper may have different answers to these questions.

In a new area of science, it is not unusual for research reports from different laboratories to conflict. Science at the cutting edge is not always clean and conclusive. This reflects both the inevitable existence of error and the possibility that all of the aspects of the problem may not yet be well understood: experiments that attempt to explore similar problems may in fact be exploring totally different aspects of a problem, and their results will appear to conflict until more experiments are done. Much of the scientific process involves the clarification of conflicts in the literature and the refinement of old ideas about the world based on new data.

Most published scientific papers probably fall somewhere on the scale between good science and ho-hum science. Some studies are more important and far-reaching in their implications than others; some have better data and fewer flaws than others; but, most of the time, they reflect an honest attempt to do good science. There are exceptions to this general rule, however. They fall into two general classes: deliberate fraud and pathological science.

Cases of documented deliberate fraud are rare and tend to make the headlines. In the field of immunology, the most famous example is that of Dr. William Summerlin, a scientist who colored black patches on his white mice in order to make it appear that they had accepted skin transplants from completely unrelated black mice. Another example comes from the field of psychology: Sir Cyril Burt, who in his time was one of the most important and influential scientists in his field, apparently fabricated thirty years worth of data purported to come from intelligence testing of identical twins. It is hard to understand why a scientist would commit fraud: the nature of science is that fraud will eventually be discovered, and the fame that the perpetrator sought will turn into notoriety and destroy his scientific reputation. Such things do happen, however, and slow the progress of science. Burt's fabrications affected psychology until after his death; Summerlin's fraud was discovered rather quickly and did less damage. Fortunately, it appears that such situations are rare.

A more subtle form of bad science is known as pathological science, after the designation of the man who first clearly identified its symptoms, the physicist Irving Langmuir. This form of bad science probably reflects self-deception (at least at first) on the part of the scientist rather than deliberate fraud. The recent controversy over Fleischmann and Pons' report of a process that apparently allowed nuclear fusion (the process that powers the sun) to occur at room temperature in a test tube can be used to illustrate pathological science. The symptoms, and their manifestation in the case of cold fusion, include:

1. Pathological science is generally performed by scientists who are not experts in the field in which they are trying to work. Fleischmann and Pons are electrochemists, not nuclear physicists, and had very little of the scientific background needed to really understand nuclear fusion.
2. The size of the effect is just above the threshold of detectability. This certainly was the case for cold fusion. Fleischmann and Pons detected a few watts of energy coming from their cold fusion cells—a factor of ten less energy would have been undetectable, while a factor of ten more energy would have been obvious to anyone. They also detected a few neutrons, indicating a nuclear process—a factor of ten fewer would have been unseen, a factor of ten more would have been obvious. These simple facts convinced most scientists at the outset that cold fusion was invalid—the amount of energy disagreed with the expected number of neutrons by a factor of 100 trillion, yet both were just above the threshold of detection.
3. The size of the effect is independent of the size of the cause. With cold fusion, doubling the size of the cell did not change the amount of heat or number of neutrons. It was later noted that the obvious control experiment (removing the suspected cause of the effect entirely by using regular water, whose normal hydrogen atoms should not undergo fusion, instead of water in which the hydrogen atoms had been substituted with deuterium atoms, as in their experiment) had not been done. When the control experiment was finally performed, the

effect did not vanish, suggesting that there was something wrong with their interpretation of the effect or that there was something funny about the effect itself.

4. Essential information about the experiment is missing. Fleischmann and Pons never published their experimental protocol, claiming that patent obligations and, later, the press of experiments, kept them from doing so. When pressed by the scientific community, they sent protocols to individual investigators trying to replicate their results, but the protocols were insufficient. Fleischmann and Pons then offered ad hoc explanations for these failures of replication; these also failed to resolve the problems.
5. The effect is totally unexpected and very important; it contradicts the available theoretical models. Cold fusion would have been a cheap, clean source of vast amounts of energy had it really existed; thus, it was a highly important effect. The possibility of its existence was in direct contradiction to the theoretical understanding of nuclear fusion current at the time (which is still the accepted understanding, incidentally), yet Fleischmann and Pons offered no new scientifically acceptable modifications of nuclear fusion theory to explain their results.
6. The number of believers soars initially to include about half of the scientific community, then declines rapidly as negative experiments pile up. It is hard to document this precisely in the case of cold fusion, but certainly the tone of editorials about it in *Science* and *Nature*, the two major general science journals, changed from initial interest, confusion, and excitement to disbelief and outright rejection quite quickly, reflecting the discussions occurring among scientists at the time.

A final topic that belongs in any discussion of bad science is the topic of pseudoscience. Pseudoscience is not science, but purports to be science. Examples include astrology, creation science, psychic surgery, and other fringe and paranormal beliefs. Pseudoscience can be distinguished from science by its inability to survive well-controlled experimental tests and by its dependence on the word of an "authority" (whether a person or a text) rather than experiment/observation/calculation. It is unfortunate that pseudoscience appears to be as attractive or more attractive to Americans than science is: *The National Enquirer* certainly has a much larger readership than does *Scientific American*, or, for that matter, *The Skeptical Inquirer*, a publication that devotes itself to scientific testing of claims of the paranormal.

Rationale for Teaching the Concept

The concept of the scientific process is not one that lends itself readily to being taught directly. Its components, however, should be taught indirectly every time any scientific concept is taught. The process itself can be incorporated into any situation in which students are expected to do hands-on science. In addition, the reasoned skepticism of a scientist approaching a new piece of information can be made a part of students' approach to scientific thinking: teaching students to ask "How do we know?" rather than "What do we know?" teaches them the essence of science. Allowing students to approach a problem as a scientist might, by educating themselves about it, formulating the problem more precisely, thinking of experiments/observations/calculations that would help to solve it, doing those tests, refining the problem some more, then ultimately presenting their work to others, helps them to understand that science is not a dead pile of facts in a textbook, but rather a living, dynamic, challenging, and exciting process. Students must learn the fundamental concepts of science, because a solid scientific knowledge base is essential for understanding not only modern science but also more general issues, such as the problems of pollution, overpopulation, resource depletion, and global warming. If this knowledge base is acquired, at least in part, as a component of an active scientific problem-solving process, students will understand it better and probably retain it longer than if they simply memorize facts from a textbook. Students that go on to do science will be better prepared for it by such experiences; those who go on to do other things will have a richer appreciation of the strengths and limitations of science. They will also have honed the thinking skills required to distinguish good science from bad science and pseudoscience, which is in itself an important and desirable result.

SUGGESTED APPLICATIONS

The scientific process can probably be best conveyed by having students approximate doing science in an inquiry learning situation with the modifications suggested in the Suggested Applications: General Considerations section of this guide. Many different topics could be covered by such an approach, including those suggested in the other concept papers in this series.

As an example, consider the problem of energy policy. This example would probably be appropriate for grades 6–8. This topic illustrates a number of the general concepts in this series, including systems (the Earth as a closed system with finite resources); change (rates of energy consumption, both by nations and by machines; rates of energy production; rate of growth of energy use); and scale (magnitudes of energy use, from that used by a light bulb to that used by a nation). Students could be told a few relevant facts to get them started, including the current fraction of oil used in the United States that is produced domestically; the amount of oil used every year by the United States and the rest of the industrial nations; the proven oil reserves for different nations of the world; and a brief history of the Persian Gulf War. They could then be asked the question "Is there a problem here?" They would then have to go through a set of group tasks:

1. Determine if a problem exists. In this case, they should be able to see that we depend heavily on foreign oil; that if the status quo continues, over a fairly short time we will depend even more heavily on foreign oil; that this situation is militarily as well as economically dangerous for the United States; and that there is, indeed, a problem. This corresponds, roughly, to steps 1–2 of the scientific process.
2. Create an exact statement of the problem. We are using up a nonrenewable resource and endangering our national security in doing so; we need to find domestic alternatives to foreign oil or to find ways to use less oil. This corresponds to step 2 of the scientific process.
3. Generate possible solutions. Exploration, conservation, alternative energy sources: these are some pretty standard suggestions for solving the problem. This step corresponds to step 3 of the scientific process, with a dose of step 1 thrown in. Students will have to educate themselves more in order to come up with possible solutions.
4. Evaluate the possible solutions. Each suggested solution should be evaluated in terms of cost and feasibility. This step, again, combines steps 1 and 3 of the scientific process.
5. Test the possible solutions directly. Here are some suggestions:
   —Students should be organized into groups, each of which will study a different suggested solution.
   —Students studying solar energy should do some experimental work with solar cells to look at their efficiency; they should then calculate the cost of land, materials, and so on needed to replace an oil-fired power plant with a solar installation; the same could be done for students advocating wind power and other alternative energy sources.
   —Students studying conservation should look experimentally at some conservation approaches. For example, they could change the thermostat setting at home for a while and see how much energy they save by doing so, or test the energy use of a more energy-

efficient light bulb, or compare the energy efficiencies of the cars belonging to the families of their classmates. How much energy does each energy-saving measure really save? What kind of effects do different conservation measures have on their lifestyle?

This step corresponds to steps 4–5 of the scientific process.

6. Communicate their results. This could be done in a seminar format (oral reports), a poster session format (each group makes a poster detailing their experiments, their results, and their conclusions, and then everyone reads everyone else's posters), or a journal format (reports are written, bound together in magazine form, and then distributed to each member of the class). A good, recent reference for this topic is:

   Hubbard, H. M. (1991). The real cost of energy. *Scientific American*, *264*, 36–42.

Scientific standards

Some sense of what good science is and is not could be conveyed by using an inquiry-based approach to evaluate pseudoscience. No sophisticated knowledge base is needed to understand some forms of pseudoscience. Astrology, for example, can be subjected to meaningful testing quite easily. Some suggestions for associated activities include:

1. Compare the forecasts of different astrologers for the same person on the same day; note similarities and differences.
2. Pass around copies of the forecasts for the day before without the labels (so that nobody knows which is for Scorpio, which for Cancer, and so on). Can people correctly pick the forecast that was supposed to apply to them? Do this for a number of days in succession, and see if they can pick their own forecast at a rate significantly higher than that predicted by chance.
3. Find out how astrologers make forecasts. Is there a standard method, or is it unreproducible from person to person?
4. Find out the theoretical basis for astrology. Does it square with what is currently known about the forces that operate in the universe, or is it scientifically inexplicable?

For other possibilities in pseudoscience testing, see back issues of *The Skeptical Inquirer* and the following books:

Gardner, M. (1957). *Fads and fallacies in the name of science*. NY: Dover Publications, Inc.

Randi, J. (1982). *Psychics, ESP, Unicorns, and other Delusions*. Buffalo, NY: Flim-Flam.

Teaching and Implementing a Problem-Based Learning Unit

Problem-based learning shares many characteristics with other inquiry-based models including those focusing on creative problem-solving. Its relationship to these other approaches is defined by differences in emphasis at various stages of the process, the nature of the discipline being studied, and how problem-based learning methodology is applied in a given setting. Whereas applications of real world problems in the medical profession (Barrows, 1985) in higher education (Chickering & Gamson, 1991) and in graduate educational administration training for principals (Bridges, 1992) can draw from a real world case perspective, utilization of the model at elementary school levels must depend to some extent on students' willingness to suspend belief around a problem presumed to be real. Thus, school-based applications of problem-based learning may still rely strongly on archetypal problems associated with learning in various subject areas. In the William and Mary science units there is an archetypal water problem, chemistry problem, ecological problem, and the like.

Problem-Based Learning as Inquiry

In what ways is problem-based learning similar to other constructivist models? Table I illustrates some key crossover features of two other commonly used models in gifted education—creative problem-solving (Parnes, 1975; Treffinger, Isaksen, & Dorval, 1994) and a more generic inquiry-based learning model (Joyce & Weil, 1996). All three models begin with a problem of some kind in various stages of disarray. In creative problem-solving, the problem emerges out of a discussion that helps determine that a problem exists through focusing on illustrations and examples and ultimately posing the problem as a question to be answered by further study. In general inquiry, the problem may be real world or not, and broad or narrow in its orientation. For example, the meaning of a given poem or the meaning of a specific war in history or finding out what happened in a specific scientific demonstration may all be the subject of inquiry-based learning. What matters is that a puzzling situation is presented (Suchman, 1964). In problem-based learning, the learner is confronted with an ill-structured problem that mirrors a real world situation, thus drawing the learner into a complex reality.

Another key feature in all of these models is the role of the teacher. In creative problem-solving she is clearly a facilitator of group process, since part of the learning to be achieved is related to the internalization of the heuristic steps in a collaborative group context. Newer versions of the model stress the naturalistic processes employed by problem solvers in the real world and thus a more flexible use of the specific steps of the strategy (Treffinger, in press). In more general inquiry models, the teacher focuses on structuring good questions, typically arranged in a careful hierarchy. The central purpose of learning is related to a specific piece of subject matter, explored at increasingly more complex levels of thought by students. The role of the teacher in problem-based learning, however, is more complex. It requires an on-going dynamic interaction with individual learners and small groups of learners to assess their level of mastery related to both content and process considerations. Questions are one form of the teaching intervention; other forms may include a new set of group activities or a self-study or a visit to a key resource person. Because the purposes of the use of the methodology are broader, the instructional component tends to be more diverse.

A third point of comparison among these three models is the focus on the learner. While each model assists the learner in developing meaning, the nature and extent of the meaning derived differs among the models. In creative problem-solving, meaning emerges from the manipulation of a prespecified and evolving process; in more traditional inquiry, meaning is derived from the careful cross-

roughage of several perspectives sifted through a set of analytical and interpretive questions. In problem-based learning, the three-part "Need to Know" board functions as the basic inquiry device. Students use it recursively to ask: What do I know, what do I need to know, and how do I find out. Meaning is derived through the in-depth reiteration of the need-to-know heuristic as the inquiry process goes on; thus it represents a holistic and integrated approach to self-learning that encourages depth and complexity of understanding.

TABLE I
DIMENSIONS OF COMPARISON AMONG CREATIVE PROBLEM-SOLVING, INQUIRY, AND PROBLEM-BASED LEARNING

Dimension	Creative Problem-solving	Inquiry	Problem-based Learning (W & M)
Nature of the problem	• Starts with a mess in which the learner seeks to understand the problem	• Confrontation with some kind of problem or puzzle	• Starts with an ill-structured problem
Role of teacher	• Role of teacher as facilitator of group process	• Role of teacher as question poser	• Role of teacher as metacognitive coach
Role of learner	• Learner constructs meaning through generating ideas	• Learner constructs meaning through questions, data collection, and analysis	• Learner constructs meaning through metacognitive and scientific heuristics
Application/ transfer	• Application to plan of action	• Application to conceptual understanding	• Application to real world policy

A final aspect for comparison among the models is represented by the application or transfer of what's learned. In creative problem-solving, the transfer is to a plan of action, worked out in detail at the level of citing potential barriers to implementing the plan and how to overcome them. In a more general inquiry framework, the application is to conceptual understanding of a set of ideas or principles that impact on an event or an artistic product. In problem-based learning, the application is intended to carry beyond process and conceptual understanding to real world utilization. Asking students to develop policy positions for real world problems and then to articulate them to relevant adult audiences is to elevate the level of learning considerably. Students have to consider the complexity inherent in real world problem resolutions, not solutions, and the inherent conflicts of various stakeholders. Thus the learning transfers directly to life.

While we can compare problem-based learning to other models of inquiry-based instruction along the dimensions just cited, it may be inappropriate to do so if it leaves readers with the impression that teachers should choose among the approaches based on their predilections and purposes. Rather, what needs to be conveyed is the sense of sophistication of utilizing problem-based learning as an overarching approach that can include creative problem-solving and more general inquiry models. Because its perspective is broad and focused on developing self-directedness in the learner, it can function quite well as an umbrella for other inquiry-based perspectives. As such, it does the most competent job of engaging the learner in constantly asking the question about her learning "What makes it important to me and my life?" For a relevancy-based curriculum, problem-based learning is a highly valuable tool.

In the William and Mary science units, problem-based learning provided an important catalyst for students' learning in three major areas. Conceptual learning about systems was addressed by infusing the problem with opportunities for students to understand interrelated social, political, economic, and scientific systems in the real world. The scientific research process was learned through an emphasis on students using experimental design techniques to tackle the scientific aspects of the problem and science content learning accrued through access to science resources that focused on specific targeted learning. Thus problem-based learning wrapped around a set of outcomes that were challenging from the start.

Implementing Problem-Based Learning in the Classroom

When implementing problem-based learning (PBL) in the classroom, it is essential to keep in mind the nature of solving ill-structured problems. The specifics of this process dictate not only the pedagogy applied, but also items such as the physical arrangement of the classroom and much of the interaction between the teacher and students.

A problem encountered in PBL is one that does not come with sufficient information to understand it well enough to make valid decisions about its causes or potential resolution. It is this characteristic of the nature of the selected problem that becomes the driving force behind the learning and the instruction. Initially, more information is essential to understand and to define the problem. As new information is gained and the problem becomes more identifiable, additional information needs to be obtained through investigating, observing, asking questions, testing and probing. Decisions of what needs to be learned, how it fits into what is already known, and how it leads to resolution of the problem are actions that require reflection, thought, and deliberation. The responsibility to bringing new information to the problem rests with students. Some of the acquired information is going to be confusing, conflicting, or ambiguous. Decisions are going to have to be made by students in spite of uncertainty. These metacognitive skills of reflection, thought, and deliberation are central to implementation of PBL. The role of the teacher is guiding group metacognition through the experience of a problem by first modeling, then practicing, refining, and ultimately having students internalize the process as a group, using it consciously independently, then finally using it individually.

The degree of assistance provided by the teacher in collecting and interpreting resources depends upon the age, experiences, and abilities of students as well as their familiarity with the subject matter involved. It is important that the teacher work through all probable directions they anticipate their students may take in defining and resolving the problem. Appropriate resources can then be identified and collected, and potentially difficult reasoning tasks are known in advance. This relates to the first of the five specific tasks for the teacher using PBL.

The teacher must keep the group process moving at all times. No phase of the learning process can be missed and each phase must be taken in order. Students are frequently ready to postulate solutions before they have an operational definition of the problem. For students to reason their way through a problem, the teacher must ensure that students use appropriate analytical reasoning skills and integrate new information they have acquired with existing knowledge at each step of the problem. Transition to each new phase of the process requires reflection, thought, and deliberation before moving on.

The second task of the teacher is to deeply probe the student's knowledge. This is probably the single most important task facing the teacher. Students must constantly be challenged to critically examine the true meaning of information or thoughts about the nature of the learning. Questions such as "Why?," "What do you mean by that?," "How do you know that's true?," "Would you explain that?," "Why do you feel that is something important for you to know?," and "What do you think that means in terms of your idea of the problem?" all serve to force students to examine in depth the matter confronting them. The teacher should guard against indicating "right" or "wrong" answers; a task that should ultimately belong to the group. Students should be challenged to further elaborate when giving appropriate responses as well as when they are not on the right track. It is only when probed enough times by the teacher that students will move toward adopting this skill as their own.

The third task is to ensure that all students are engaged in the group process. Depending on the size of the group and the personalities involved, this can be a difficult job. Some students feel comfortable in a small group, but are very hesitant in front of a large group. Getting these children to contribute important ideas and to engage in cognitive interaction with their peers is difficult but critical to the group as well as to the process of PBL. Common strategies already used in the classroom such as expectant looks, ample wait time, and simple questions such as "Who has thoughts on this?," and directly asking reluctant students to share important information that you know they have can help to get all of students involved. Often reluctant students will be comfortable speaking for their small group, feeling the support from their group members.

Another critical task is to maintain an ongoing educational diagnosis of each student as well as the whole group, particularly of reasoning difficulties and understanding acquired information. The use of probing questions together with other assessments should disclose areas of difficulty so that appropriate remediation can take place. At times it will be effective to "step out" of the problem to address a reasoning strategy, while at other times it may be more effective to address it as a "need to know." Ongoing diagnosis will also allow the teacher to incorporate labs and demonstrations that can assist student understanding of newly acquired information. Authentic assessments built into the problem scenario are particularly helpful to ensure a complete diagnosis.

The final task is to modulate the level of challenge of the problem. It is important that an appropriate level of creative tension be present throughout the experience. The level of challenge can be addressed at both the total group level as well as the small group level. Specific areas of investigation can be assigned to appropriate groups in order to meet differing academic or intellectual needs of students. A particularly difficult phase of the problem may need to be followed by a less intense experience to allow time for reorganization and a needed break from the routine.

Understanding and consistent adherence to these tasks of the teacher is imperative for the success of PBL. It is important for the personal dynamics of the group to be established early in the experience. If our goal is to enhance the self sufficiency of our students and to promote independent thinkers and learners, it is important that we avoid the dependence of the group on the teacher. The teacher as facilitator must evolve from modeling, coaching, to fading throughout the problem. The teacher must at first model the thinking process for the group. Frequent metacognitive challenges must be made of students. An accurate reasoning process must be presented to students if we ultimately want them to reason effectively. Searching for appropriate resources is a critical part of problem finding and solving. The frustration and difficulty in locating and understanding information is a real part of the process. Initially, the teacher must convey that professionals often go through the same difficulty.

Coaching becomes the next phase of the teaching; stepping in to question when it is apparent that a step has been missed, regaining the focus of the group when it begins to wander, and stepping in to lend assistance when confusion overcomes the group. The amount and duration of intervention will be dictated by the level of difficulty, ability, and age of students, and the development rate of the group dynamics.

Ultimately the teacher wants to be able to fade into the background, allowing the group to operate independently. This may be done physically, with the teacher moving out of the line of sight of students, or may be accomplished by lessening the degree of involvement in daily dynamics of the group. At various times in the problem the teacher will move into and out of all three of these roles: modeling, coaching and fading. Figure I on the following page demonstrates the problem movement from an instructional perspective.

Getting Started

The first day of implementing PBL in your classroom in all likelihood will be one of apprehension and uncertainly on the part of both the teacher and students. It is imperative that the teacher projects enthusiasm and excitement about the process to students and makes it clear to them that it will probably be different than what they are accustomed to in a classroom setting. It is likewise imperative that the teacher is prepared for a somewhat different classroom climate. It may take time for both students and teacher to feel fully comfortable in new roles; however, the excitement and rewards that both will share as a result of PBL will develop in short order.

After establishing agreement on objectives and responsibilities of the group and the teacher, the problem should be presented and the process engaged immediately. The "Need to Know" board is a crucial item in the room. It will serve as an organizer and focus for the group throughout the problem. It is a visual reminder of the process and aids in engagement each day as well as closure at the end of each session. It should be devoted solely to the problem and should be located in a central position where it is visible to all. Depending on the age of students, it may be appropriate for the teacher to record on the board or it may be the responsibility of students. If the teacher is the recorder, it is critical that the information written on the board if directly from students; not filtered or altered by the teacher. Clarification of what the student has said may be necessary, as well as confirmation that what was recorded accurately portrays what the student meant. All three of the item headings "What we know," "What we need to know," and "Where we can find out" will remain on the board with the specifics evolving as the problem evolves. "Where we can find out" is probably more appropriate for elementary aged students until they have experience with research skills and resource gathering.

Students should be seated so that they can see both the "Need to Know" board and each other. A "U" shaped arrangement may facilitate the face-to-face interaction that PBL encourages. This arrangement needs to be flexible however, to accommodate easy movement to small group seating where students can focus on their group mates. Arrangements need to be made in the room to accommodate a resource center that can be accessible to students and an area that can accommodate ongoing experiments and demonstrations so that time is not unnecessarily spent daily setting and taking down equipment. Responsibility for both of these areas should be given to students except when there are safety concerns.

If the process employed in PBL is different from what your students have experienced, it is helpful to inform parents of the goals and objectives of the problem, as well as an overview of the mechanics you will employ in the classroom. After the problem is under way and group dynamics have developed, you may want to invite parents into the room as observers to see the nature of the intellectual interaction that is such a strength of the process. Periodic parent updates on the progress of the problem can be written by students as both an assessment tool and a means of communication with home. This can serve as a catalyst for significant interaction at home as well. Often it gives students an opportunity to express thoughts and ideas at home, making them more comfortable contributing to the group process. Parents will likely be eager participants as an audience to the final problem resolution if they are informed and included in the process.

Figure I
Structure of Problem Movement
Problem-Based Learning: Problem Diagnosis and Solution Building

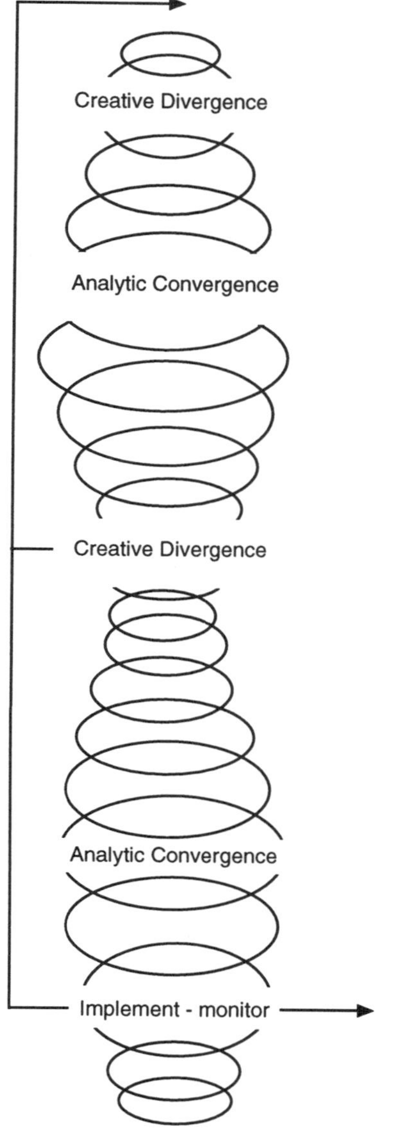

Ill-structured problem is presented

- What is going on?
- What do we know?
- How can we find out?
- Where does the information lead us?
- Do we have enough information?
- Is the information reliable?
- What's the problem?

Problem is represented

Problem is presented

- What should we know about it?
- What do we know?
- What do we need to know?
- How can we find out?
- Do we have enough information?
- Is the information reliable?
- Where does the information lead us?
- What's a solution?

Solution(s) is/are represented

- What solution fits best?

Similarly, it is important to include administrators in the problem so they better understand the significant outcomes of the unit, rather than observing an isolated lesson or two without knowledge of the entire process. Administrators can also be asked to help the student evaluate their work on the problem, enhancing the relationship and interaction with their students.

When cognitive interaction is valued and encouraged, and students are at the center of the learning process, group dynamics will result in a charged atmosphere where ideas, thoughts, and concepts are freely debated and argued modeling the nature of interaction of practicing scientists and other professionals. The resulting climate may be quite different from what teachers, students and administrators are accustomed to. As with practicing professionals, ground rules must be established and adhered to, but should enhance, not interfere with, the creative process or with meaningful cognitive interaction between individuals. If the school culture and the surrounding are traditional, teacher centered, quiet and still, the PBL classroom will be in contrast, but hopefully not in conflict with others. Administrators and colleagues need to be aware of the goals and objectives of what you are doing in your room and certainly aware of the benefits to your students. Regular observation by an administrator of the group dynamics of your students and awareness of the significant learning outcomes should help to make your administration strong advocates for PBL.

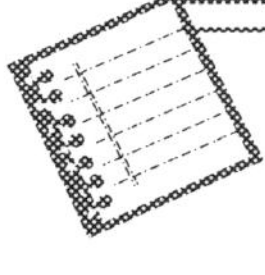

IMPLEMENTING EXPERIMENTAL DESIGN IN A PROBLEM-BASED LEARNING CONTEXT

Teaching experimental design is an important part of teaching science in general and is an integral part of teaching the William and Mary problem-based units. Science is a process, not a pile of textbook facts, and it is desirable for students to experience the scientific process as directly as possible. Every child should have the excitement of asking a question of nature and receiving an intelligible answer, and every citizen should have some feeling for how the "experts" arrive at their knowledge.

A clear distinction should be drawn between experimental design and hands-on experimentation. Experimental design is the phase of the scientific process in which the scientific problem is defined, an appropriate method for solving the problem is developed, and the experiment (or observation or calculation) is *planned*. Hands-on experimentation (or observation or calculation) is the phase of the scientific process in which the planned method is actually carried out. In order for students to fully understand the scientific process, it is desirable for them to both plan and perform their own experiments.

With the above distinction in mind, it becomes clear that most curriculum approaches fail to teach experimental design. Many curriculum packages do not allow students to participate in the experimental design phase at all. Although there are hands-on opportunities provided, the students simply follow the instructions provided and may not ever need to understand why they did what they did. Other curriculum approaches address this problem by teaching students formal experimental design nomenclature, data collection and analysis techniques, and presentation strategies. In many of these situations, however, the student's motivation for creating and performing an experiment is not the true scientific "In order to answer a question" but rather the pedagogical "The teacher says we have to do an experiment." This approach (unintentionally) subverts the scientific process by disconnecting experimentation from its true purpose, namely, the intentional acquisition of particular knowledge about the world. While it may be important for students to learn how to conduct an experiment, it is even more important for them to understand why people bother to do experiments at all.

Problem-based learning provides a new and somewhat different opportunity for teaching experimental design. In problem-based learning, experimentation is driven by a need to acquire new information relevant to the solution of the problem posed by the unit. This is appealing from a teacher's perspective because it is much closer to a real scientist's reason for doing an experiment: experimentation is driven by the need to know the result. This is also highly motivational for students: they aren't designing AN experiment (any experiment) just to please the teacher or to win the science fair, they're designing experiments whose results will help them solve the real-life problem posed by the unit. For the students, experimental design thus becomes relevant.

QUESTIONING STRATEGIES FOR FACILITATING EXPERIMENTAL DESIGN IN THE PROBLEM-BASED CLASSROOM

In the course of a problem-based science unit, experimental design can be taught in a variety of ways, depending on the nature of the scientific questions involved and the ages and abilities of the students in the class. Because the teacher acts as a metacognitive coach and facilitator rather than as a lecturer, the standard lecture format is probably not appropriate. Rather, the teacher must have a good grasp of the fundamentals of experimental design and guide the students toward the design of good experiments through appropriate questioning. Questions that will help to guide the students include:

1. **Brainstorming Questions**
   —What is the question we're trying to answer?
   —Why is this an important question?
   —How will the answer to this question help us to solve the problem posed by the unit?
   —What could we do to answer this question?
   —How would a student-proposed experiment answer the question?
   —What do we expect will happen in a student-proposed experiment?
   —Why do we predict this?
2. **Practical Questions**
   —Is the proposed experiment feasible or not?
   —What materials would we need in order to try a student-proposed experiment?
   —What materials do we have available?
   —Can we do the student-proposed experiment given what we have?
   —Which experimental approach is the best, given the materials and time we have?
3. **Planning Questions**
   —How can we be sure that our experiment is giving us the right answer (What are our controls?)?
   —What do we need to change to get our answer and why? (What is our independent variable?)
   —What has to stay the same during our experiment and why? (What are our constants?)
   —What data need to be collected and why? (What are the dependent variables that we will survey?)
   —How can we make sure that we don't accidentally foul up and confuse ourselves? (Repeated trials)

—How are we going to record the data?
—How do we plan to analyze the data?
—What are the steä3 we're going to follow in order to do the experiment?

4. **Debriefing Questions**
   —What happened in the experiment?
   —Did our prediction turn out to be correct?
   —Is our answer good enough, or do we need to do more experiments or data analysis to make it better?
   —If we were going to do the experiment again, how would we change it to make it work better?
   —Does our answer raise new questions?
   —Does our answer help us solve the problem posed in the unit?

The questions listed above have been organized into groups, each of which is useful at a different stage of the experimental design process.

Brainstorming

The first phase of this process is the brainstorming phase, in which students define the scientific question to be answered and decide on some general experimental approaches that could be used. In this phase, it is important to keep the students on track with respect to the scientific question being approached and to its relevance to the solution of the problem posed by the unit. The questions "What is the scientific question we're trying to answer?" and "How will this answer help us to solve the problem (the ill-structured problem posed by the unit)?" should be repeated as frequently as seems necessary. It is important to have the "Need to Know" board for the unit available to the students during this process. Frequent reference to the questions on the board will help to keep appropriate scientific questions at the forefront of discussion. The discussion should be otherwise unconstrained, in order to elicit the widest variety of ideas from the students and to explore these ideas in detail. Because of this, no reference should be made to the availability of materials or the practicality of proposed techniques: this comes later, in the practical questions phase.

Practical Questions

The practical questions phase brings the students down to reality and forces them to decide which of the experimental approaches that they have discussed are actually feasible given the available materials and resources. During this phase, students should be shown the materials suggested for the lesson and allowed to decide whether other materials are necessary and can be acquired. Plans for their acquisition should be made at this time. This phase can be used to force the students to select an experimental approach from the available possibilities. It may be that different groups of students will feel strongly about the merits of different approaches; if multiple approaches are feasible given the available time and materials, the different groups should be encouraged to proceed separately with their different methods. This will provide an important reality check for the eventual answer. If both approaches really address the same question, than the answer should be the same regardless of the approach used.

Planning

In the planning phase, the students plan their experimental manipulations in detail. Questions in this phase include questions that guide the students toward picking appropriate variables, constants, and controls; planning all experimental steps; and deciding on how to collect and analyze data. At the end of this phase, students should have a written protocol for their experiment (a list of all steps to be taken during the experiment) and should also have made blank data tables in which to record their results and observations. Once this step is complete (and not before!), students can perform the hands-on manipulations that constitute their experiment.

The planning phase can be facilitated using formal experimental design terminology if the students have already been exposed to it or if the teacher feels that it is useful to use this terminology in order to introduce it to students; this terminology is not essential, however. It is important for teachers to know that, as a rule, most of the formal experimental design terms are not commonly used by scientists in planning or in discussing their work. The only exception to this is the word "control," because controls are often the most important aspect of an experiment. If the formal experimental design words get in the way of student intuition or understanding, they should not be stressed. It is more important that students know that it is important to change only one thing at a time than that they be able to define the term "independent variable."

Debriefing

The debriefing phase, even though it occurs after the experiment has been performed, is still an integral part of the experimental design process. Without this phase, the students have no way of assessing their experiments and learning from their experiences. Debriefing questions include questions designed to assess whether the experiment worked as expected and what the results mean. Other questions allow students to reflect on the design and planning of the experiment and to assess what worked and what didn't. They can then decide how they would change things to make the experiment run more smoothly. In addition, students are asked to list new questions raised by the experiment and its results. This emphasizes the cyclic and expanding nature of the scientific process, as each experiment generates more questions than it solves. Finally, students are asked whether the results are relevant to the problem posed by the unit, thus reemphasizing the reason for performing the experiment in the first place.

Developmental issues

Experimental design should be handled in a way that is appropriate to the ability and age of the student. Hands-on experimentation is a part of the native repertoire of human beings, as anyone who has ever watched a toddler play can testify. Young children naturally manipulate objects and discover their properties in a trial-and-error fashion. As children mature, they become capable of defining increasingly sophisticated questions about the world and of using increasingly sophisticated approaches to their solution. This change is reflected by the experiments suggested in the problem-based units. The scientific questions addressed by these experiments should be resolvable by high-ability children at the grade level suggested for the unit.

EXAMPLES

INFORMAL EXPERIMENTAL DESIGN

The least formal type of hands-on experience found in the units involves relatively unstructured, trial-and error exposure to a new experience or concept. This type of experience can be used from kindergarten on; it can be appropriate even for adults, depending on the nature of the question to be answered. In the upper elementary unit "Acid, Acid Everywhere," the first experimental activity, named "Playing with pH," serves to introduce students rapidly to the pH scale and to the properties of pH paper. In this activity, students are introduced to pH paper and allowed to investigate its properties as they test a variety of safe household liquids.

In this kind of activity, formal experimental design nomenclature and procedures are unnecessary: all that is really needed is proper planning and preparation. Students need to agree on rules for handling the materials safely, and to write a simple protocol describing the steps that they will take to use the materials. This is probably best done as a class, with the teacher writing the safety rules and the protocol in a place where all students can see them. The teacher can demonstrate proper use of pH paper in order to facilitate the protocol-writing step. Before the students begin the activity, they should also construct a data table, so that they will remember to record their data in an appropriate place during the experiment. Appropriate questions from the list above, and appropriate answers, thus include:

1. **Brainstorming Questions**
   —What is the question we're trying to answer? Why is pH paper useful? We know that the hazardous materials workers at the spill site used it to test the stuff dripping from the truck. Why?
   —What could we do to answer this question? Use it on a range of liquids and see the results.
2. **Practical Questions**
   —What materials do we need for the experiment? *(pH paper, safe liquids)*
   —What materials do we have available? *(pH paper, safe liquids, containers, paper towels)*
3. **Experimental Design Questions**
   —What are the steps we're going to follow in order to do the experiment? *(Dip the pH paper in the liquid, drain the extra liquid, then compare the pH paper's color to the chart on the side of the box; write down the number of the closest color match.)*
4. **Follow-up Questions**
   —What happened in the experiment? *(Different liquids gave us different numbers.)*
   —If we were going to do the experiment again, how would we change it to make it work better? *(Answers will vary, depending on exactly how the experiment went.)*
   —Does our answer raise new questions? *(What do the numbers mean? What was the number of the stuff at the spill? What happens if you mix liquids that have different pH values? What is pH, anyway?)*
   —Does our answer help us solve the problem posed in the unit? *(If the workers thought pH was important, we need to find out their results and decide what they mean to us; in order to understand the results, we need to know what pH is . . . but at least we know how to measure it now, and what the pH values of some ordinary liquids are.)*

The "Playing with pH" activity is most efficiently handled as a planned trial-and-error activity; belaboring formal experimental design ideas in the planning phase is not necessary. As written, the activity described in the unit has most formal experimental design elements. If every lab group in the class tests every substance, repeated trials are built into the process; constants include the liquids being tested, the pH paper, and the testing method; the independent variable is the liquid being tested; and the dependent variable is the pH value obtained. While there are no controls built into the process, they are not necessary for this exploratory activity. If the students have encountered formal experimental design in the past, they could list the elements of experimental design that are present in the activity, but this is not necessary in order to answer the question addressed by the hands-on work. This is true for many of the experiments suggested in the units: it is important for the teacher to pay attention to the experimental design elements, but it is not always necessary for the students, as long as the teacher is available to ask the planning questions suggested above and to coach the process along.

FORMAL EXPERIMENTAL DESIGN

While many of the experimental activities suggested in the units can be used without resorting to explicit attention to formal experimental design principles and terminology, others can be profitably experienced at a more formal level. These opportunities are important for developmentally advanced high-ability students in the upper elementary grades and for all students using the units at the middle school level. An example of an experimental activity that can be presented in a formal context is Lesson 10 from the unit "Acid, Acid Everywhere," entitled "The Effect of Acid on Plants." In this activity, the students try to answer the question of the possible effect of the acid spill on the organisms in the creek ecosystem by experimenting with the effects of vinegar (a known, safe acid) on the growth and appearance of potted plants.

Appropriate experimental design questions, and some answers, for each phase of this activity include:

1. **Brainstorming Questions**
   - —What is the question we're trying to answer? *(How does acid affect plants?)*
   - —Why is this an important question? *(If we know the answer, we can predict what the acid spill might do to the creek ecosystem.)*
   - —How will the answer to this question help us to solve the problem posed by the unit? *(Same answer as above.)*
   - —What could we do to answer this question? *(Water plants with acid and see what happens.)*
   - —What do we expect will happen in this experiment? *(The acid will change the appearance or growth pattern of the plants.)*
   - —Why do we predict this? *(Acid is pretty strong stuff.)*
2. **Practical Questions**
   - —Is the proposed experiment feasible or not? *(Depends on what the students propose)*
   - —What materials would we need in order to try the experiment? *(Depends on what they propose)*
   - —What materials do we have available? *(Those listed in the unit)*
   - —Can we do the experiment given what we have? *(Depends on what the students propose)*
   - —Which experimental approach is the best, given the materials and time we have? *(Depends on what the students propose)*

3. **Planning Questions**
   —How can we be sure that our experiment is giving us the right answer? What are our controls? *(Plants watered with water rather than acid should be our standard for what "normal" looks like: if they start looking funny, we're in trouble . . .)*
   —What do we need to change to get our answer? What is our independent variable?, and why? *(What the plant is watered with: we might want to vary the acid concentration, because maybe there's a threshold that needs to be passed before we see an effect.)*
   —What has to stay the same during our experiment? What are our constants?, and why? *(Type of plants, pots, soil, watering frequency and amount, exposure to sunlight. It is probably important to do the test and the controls simultaneously . . .)*
   —What data need to be collected? What are our dependent variables?, and why? *(We need to make observations about the appearance of the plants and to measure their height/ number and size of leaves or whatever at regular intervals.)*
   —How can we make sure that we don't accidentally foul up and confuse ourselves? *(Repeated trials) (Multiple plants watered with each different concentration of acid.)*
   —How are we going to record the data? *(Set up a data table in advance.)*
   —How do we plan to analyze the data? *(Compare the appearance and height of the treated and untreated plants. Students could do statistical analysis on the height, if desired, but that's advanced for upper elementary!)*
   —What are the steps we're going to follow in order to do the experiment? *(Students write this.)*

4. **Follow-up questions**
   —What happened in the experiment? *(The plants watered with the highest concentrations of vinegar turned yellow and died.)*
   —Did our prediction turn out to be correct? *(Yes)*
   —Is our answer good enough, or do we need to do more experiments or data analysis to make it better? *(Will depend on the protocol used . . .)*
   —If we were going to do the experiment again, how would we change it to make it work better? *(Will depend on the protocol used . . .)*
   —Does our answer raise new questions? *(Are different kinds of plants more tolerant/ less tolerant of acid conditions than the ones we used? Do different acids have different effects? How would HCl affect our plants?)*
   —Does our answer help us solve the problem posed in the unit? *(It looks as though too much acid is bad for plants, so it may be that letting the acid flow into the creek will damage the creek ecosystem. Because lower concentrations of acid seem to affect plants less than do higher concentrations, if the HCl was diluted enough, it might be safe to let it flow into the creek. Maybe adding lots of water to the spill to dilute it will help, not hurt.)*

This activity is best handled in a formal way because an experiment planned with explicit attention to controls, constants, and repeated trials will be much more likely to definitively answer the question. If the students neglect the normal control, then they won't be able to answer the question "How do you know that the plants wouldn't have died or turned yellow anyway?" If they neglect repeated trials and their one acid-watered plant gets upended one night by the custodian, their experiment is lost. The debriefing process at the end of the activity will be very important for such an experiment. Something is bound to fail and confuse the issue, and the first time through, no protocol will be perfect. This is an important lesson for the students to learn: failure can be instructive.

This activity could be used as an introduction to formal experimental design nomenclature for students who have never encountered it or as a recall exercise for students who have seen formal experimental design nomenclature before. It is not absolutely necessary to use the formal nomenclature, although appropriate questioning, as outlined above, can be used to facilitate appropriate experimental design. In any case, it is very important for the teacher to be sure that the experimental protocol arrived upon by the students contains all of the appropriate experimental design elements.

Monitoring and Assessing Student Progress

The teacher has many opportunities to monitor and assess student participation and progress during and after the experimental activities in the problem-based units.

In-Progress Monitoring

Because of the teacher's role as facilitator of problem-based learning, it is important for the teacher to be aware of the participation of individual students and to attempt to elicit contributions from all students. While the activity is in progress, the teacher should actively monitor individual student participation, both by observing the students as they work and by reading the students' problem logs and experimental design worksheets.

Product Assessment

Every experiment performed in the problem-based context should result in a final product. Usually it will be either a formal lab write-up (for example, a completed lab report form) or an in-class presentation. The teacher should be grading the experimental write-up/presentation based on the following criteria:

1. The purpose of the experiment and its relevance to the unit problem should be clearly stated.
2. The description of the experiment should be complete enough that someone else could repeat the experiment, given the materials that the student used.
3. The experiment should have been designed correctly; all necessary experimental design elements should be present. Important elements for most experiments include controls, appropriate constants, a single independent variable, repeated trials to establish each data point, and appropriate data collection. (In the acid/plants experiment outlined above, the controls are the plants watered with water only; constants include the plants, pots, soil, and growth conditions. The single thing that is changed is the concentration of vinegar in the water used to water the plants; and multiple plants would be used to establish each data point.)
4. The conclusions drawn at the end of the experiment should be supported by the data.
5. The data analysis and presentation should be appropriate and clear.
6. The implications of the results of the experiment for the solution of the unit problem should be clearly described.

Summary

Teaching experimental design in a problem-based context differs from teaching it in a traditional setting because the role of the teacher is different. Acting as a facilitator, the teacher can guide the students through the experimental design process with appropriate questioning techniques. Students can thus be helped to both design and perform experiments whose results are relevant to the solution of the ill-structured real-world problem posed by the unit. In the process, their investigation skills will be enhanced.

TEACHER BACKGROUND AND RESOURCES

In order for a teacher to teach the principles of formal experimental design effectively, it is necessary for that teacher to know them herself. For many teachers, this is a daunting problem. Fortunately, there is a good resource available: the book *Students and Research*, by Julia H. Cothron, Ronald N. Giese, and Richard J. Rezba (Kendall/Hunt, 1986). This book explores formal experimental design in careful detail with many good examples for all grade levels (K–12.) For a teacher who doesn't know an independent variable from a control, it is a very useful introduction to both the terminology and the applications of experimental design.

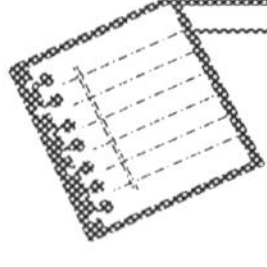

APPROPRIATE USE OF LABORATORY ACTIVITIES IN SCIENCE PROGRAMS

Good laboratory experiences can open up new areas of science for a student, illustrate processes that can only be described inadequately by a textbook, and give a student the fundamentals of experimental design and scientific proof. For these reasons, scientists and science educators want their students to participate in as many good laboratory experiences as possible. The William and Mary units contain several of these experiences.

Moreover, there are many different commercially available curriculum packages that include laboratory work. They range from the standard basal text materials to small, innovative enrichment packages. The types of laboratory experiences that these curriculum packages contain can be sorted into a number of different categories, as described below:

1. Dry labs: labs which mimic scientific processes without using scientifically appropriate materials: examples would include modeling the behavior of meiotic chromosomes with bits of string, making baking soda volcanoes, or comparing gummi worms with nightcrawlers.
2. Labs whose entire purpose is teaching the proper use of equipment; for example, labs entitled "Introduction to the Microscope" or "Metric Measurements."
3. Recipe labs: examples would include the standard chemistry labs which basically ask "if you add X to Y, what happens?"
4. Observation labs: dissecting a frog, observing the phases of the moon, looking at slides of onion root tips to observe mitotic chromosomes.
5. Question labs: labs which pose a scientific question and address it experimentally.
6. Open-ended experiences: lab experiences which don't allow the student to merely follow a protocol but, rather, require him to design and perform an appropriate experiment to test a hypothesis that he has made some contribution to developing. Such lab experiences can be part of elaborate critical thinking packages or can be simple one-liners that begin with such words as "Design an experiment . . . " or "What if?"

Some generalizations can be made about the intrinsic scientific value of labs in these different categories which are listed in ascending order of merit:

- Most dry labs are a nonproductive way to use class time. They do not really pose a scientific question; the materials used bear no relation to the actual process; students do not even get to observe something real. If you think that going through the motions would be fun for students or reinforce something that they've learned in the text, have them do these labs at home for extra points.
- The scientific value of many learning-to-use-equipment labs may also be minimal. While a several-day lab session devoted to the proper use of the microscope is fully justifiable for middle school students, a full day lab session devoted to teaching them to use a metric ruler is probably not, as they could pick up this skill in a question lab experience just as well. The material presented in such labs could be included in a recipe lab, observation lab, question lab, or open-ended lab experience equally well, and presenting it in such a context will probably enhance student motivation to learn it.
- Recipe labs used in moderation are all right, particularly in such situations as chemistry class where you don't want to have the safety problems that flow from students experimenting on their own: they still get to observe real chemical behavior. In addition, these labs teach students to follow a scientific protocol, which is a valuable scientific skill.
- Observation labs are great if students know what they're looking for beforehand. If they're prepared, the observations will enhance their understanding of the phenomenon they're supposed to observe. Some provision should be made to encourage them to note as many features of the system they're observing as possible. New insights about cell structure may hit them while they're only supposed to be looking for mitotic chromosomes in onion root tip cells, for example.
- Question labs are potentially very valuable. They offer the student a window into the solution of a scientific problem. There are some excellent curriculum materials available that provide good question lab experiences. Unfortunately, most question labs (particularly those in basal curricula) look like recipe labs: the student is given a list of materials and instructions for her manipulation, but not encouraged to develop the scientific question on her own or to participate in the experimental design phase. As a result, the student frequently does not understand the purpose or design of the experiment that she performs, and the scientific process component of such labs is lost. As the curriculum world is loaded with this sort of question lab, perhaps the best thing to do is to convert canned question labs into more open-ended laboratory experiences. Open-ended experiences necessarily take more time than do canned question labs, because students have to think about what they're going to do before they do it. If even a few such canned labs are converted into open-ended experiences during a school semester, though, the net effect will be positive. An example of such a conversion is included below.
- Open-ended laboratory experiences are the closest approximation to doing real science that a student is likely to have. It is worth omitting unimportant recipe labs, dry labs, and in-class textbook reading exercises in order to squeeze in the time for these things in class. The standard way of including such experiences has been to make the student do them alone as an outside project or as a science fair project. While open-ended laboratory experiments may be preferable for several reasons, there are also problems associated with this approach.
- It's just as hard for the student to make time for such activities outside class as it is for the teacher to do it in class. Such projects are often left to the last minute and done poorly.

- The process of doing science goes very slowly in isolation. A student working alone or with another classmate but without much adult input will not get very far and the process will be depressing and frustrating.
- The competitive aspects of science fairs often force the student to pay more attention to appearance than to substance: the neatness of the poster and its dimensions are often stressed far more than the soundness of the student's experimental design or the originality of his ideas.
- Competition is also a real turn-off for many students, particularly for science-prone ones who have learned that it's a lot safer to keep a low profile than to arouse the envy of their classmates, or for girls who think it's socially inappropriate to appear smart. While real science does have competitive aspects, the reality is that most of a scientist's work occurs in collaboration with other scientists. This is both enjoyable and productive, but it is not an element in most science fair experiences.

In order to integrate open-ended experiences into the classroom in a productive way, it is necessary both to allocate class time for such experiences and to monitor the different stages that students go through in a careful way.

Example: Uncanning the Experiment

Converting a canned question lab into a more hands- and brains-on process for the student is relatively staightforward, although it demands a bit of preparation. Don't just hand the student the lab worksheet and have him follow it. In fact, never give the student the prepared lab worksheet. Instead, pose the problem for students in a pre-lab class session and have them figure out how to solve it or, even better, try and start them on the path to defining the problem themselves. This will necessarily take more time than doing a canned experiment, which is why you need to dispense with the less important parts of the curriculum.

The following is an example of how this might be done. Suppose the canned experiment is the following:

Investigating Light's Effect on Plants

In this experiment, you will investigate the effect of light on plants.

Materials and Equipment

Eighteen marigold seeds
Potting soil
Six three inch plant pots
Six coffee cans with tops and bottoms removed
Five coffee can lids with holes cut out of their centers, covered with cellophane of the following colors: clear, red, yellow, blue, green
One intact dark plastic coffee can lid
Cafeteria tray
Paper towels
Water

Procedure

1. Fill each plant pot with potting soil (to a point one inch below the rim).
2. Plant three marigold seeds in each pot, one quarter inch deep and spaced as far as possible apart from each other.
3. Cover each coffee can with one of the prepared lids.
4. Cover the cafeteria tray with a one inch deep layer of paper towels. Place the plant pots on the tray. Water each pot well. Place one coffee can over each plant pot.
5. Put the tray in a well-lit place. Add water to the tray so that the paper towels stay quite wet. Leave the setup alone for three weeks, but make sure that the paper towels stay wet.
6. Remove each coffee can and observe the marigolds underneath. What color are the plants under each coffee can? Measure the height of each plant and record it in your data table.

Questions

1. How did the plants grown under different colors of light differ?
2. Were there any similarities between plants grown in the dark and plants grown under some colors of light?
3. If you were a nurseryman, what kind of light would you want in your greenhouse?

A canned lab can be made more open-ended by following the series of steps described below.

I. Introduce the Topic

In this step, you assemble the key concepts needed to understand and provide a rationale for the laboratory experience to follow.

The lab in this example was designed to fit into either a photosynthesis unit or into a plant tropisms unit. The in-class introduction to this lab could begin by having students tell you what they know about light and plants. The important facts that they raise (for example, plants grow towards the light, plants use light energy to make their food) should be written on the board and discussed as they are raised. Once the knowledge base has been assembled, students will be primed for the next step in this process.

II. Pose the Scientific Problem

This should be done as indirectly as possible, so that students will have a reasonable opportunity to figure out what the problem is on their own. In this case, instead of telling students that they will be observing the effects of different colors of light on plants, you could hand each lab group a prism, and have them put it in sunlight and watch the rainbow appear. Ask them to describe the rainbow and tell you what its appearance says about the nature of sunlight. At this point, you can either try to indirectly elicit the key question for the experiment or ask students directly: do they think that plants need all of the colors of light or only a few? After some opinions are proffered and evaluated by the group.

III. Design, Refine, and Run the Experiment

Break the class into lab groups (four students per group is a good number). Ask them to think about how they could experimentally find out the answer to the question. Give them some time to brainstorm as lab groups, then collect their suggestions and write the important points up on the board. Discuss the key components for such an experiment: plants, sources of different colors of light, conditions that permit plant growth.

Now, dig out the prepared coffee can lids, plant pots, and so on, and ask students in each lab group to design an experiment to test the effect of different colors of light on plants using these materials. Let them brainstorm and write down their protocol; then go over each group's protocol with them and evaluate it. Make sure that they have included the "full sunlight" control and the "no sunlight" test experiment and that they understand why these things are important; make sure that they have multiple seeds in each pot and understand why this is necessary. Ask them what provision their plants will have for water; ask them whether or not it's a good idea for the coffee cans to be removed once a day to water the plants. Also make sure that they have some idea of how they will evaluate their results: for example, they should have planned to observe the color and size of their plants, measure their heights, and so on. Once a lab group has come up with a reasonable protocol, have them set up the experiment and run it. The precise experimental design may vary from lab group to lab group; as long as their protocols look reasonable, let each lab group follow its own protocol.

IV. Collect and Evaluate the Data

After the experiments have been run, have students collect their data, evaluate their results, and attempt to answer the initial scientific question based on their results. If their data don't answer the question, have them explain why this is so and suggest modifications to their original protocol that would allow them to attack the question better. In class, discuss their results; also discuss differences (if any) in the results of lab groups that followed different protocols. Attempt to account for these differences.

V. Generalize from the Results of Their Experiments

In class, ask students what questions are raised by their experimental results and list them on the board. Possibilities for this lab include:

1. Why are plants raised in the dark lighter in color than plants raised in the light?
2. Why are the internode distances in plants raised in the dark or in certain colors of light longer than those of plants grown in full sunlight?
3. Common wisdom says that plants grow towards the light. Why did the plants grown in the dark grow up rather than down or sideways?
4. Can we narrow down the frequencies of light to which plants respond?
5. Are the frequencies required for green color different from those required for short internode distances?

For the most interesting questions, ask the group to suggest experimental approaches that would help to resolve the question. If a really interesting question comes up and someone really wants to solve it, help him design an experiment and run it outside of class, then report his results in class.

In the post-lab class discussion, be sure to have students answer the questions raised in the original lab questions section if they look worthwhile; also pose open-ended ones of your own. (For example, on a planet circling the star Betelgeuse, sunlight is red. What would marigold plants grown in such sunlight look like?)

While the material presented in both approaches to this laboratory investigation is the same, students will have participated much more effectively here than they would have by merely following the original canned lab protocol. Many canned question labs can be uncanned in this way; the only real limitations are those posed by safety and time.

Implementation of Teacher-Facilitated Experimental Design

In the William and Mary units, an overall approach to teacher-facilitated experimental design has been incorporated into each of the lessons that require this method. Students are first primed to approach the topic by teacher-led discussion of issues relevant to an aspect of the problem that can be approached by an appropriate experiment. Then, students are shown a collection of available materials and asked to think about ways in which they might approach the answer to the scientific question posed in the initial discussion. They are given a Student Brainstorming Worksheet which asks questions designed to guide their thinking about possible experiments to answer the problem.

After the initial brainstorming session, students are asked to fill out a Student Experiment Worksheet. This worksheet forces them to think about the nuts and bolts of a good experiment: variables, constants, controls, repeated trials, and so on.

After students have planned the intellectual details of their experiment, they are asked to write a protocol detailing their planned materials, methods, and data to be collected. The Student Protocol Worksheet provides structure for this process.

Once the protocol has been written and checked, students can proceed with their experiment. Data should be collected and recorded; analysis of the results should be performed; and the results are then written up using the Laboratory Report form and incorporated into the problem log. In-class discussion helps students in the interpretation of their results and in the understanding of their implications for the unit's problem-based problem.

A teacher brainstorming sheet might look like this:

1. What do we need to find out? (the scientific question)

   We need to find out how different colors of light affect the growth of plants.

2. What materials are available?

   Eighteen marigold seeds

   Potting soil

   Six three inch plant pots

   Six coffee cans with tops and bottoms removed

   Five coffee can lids with holes cut out of their centers, covered with cellophane of the following colors: clear, red, yellow, blue, green

   One intact dark plastic coffee can lid

   Cafeteria tray

   Paper towels

   Water

3. How can we use the materials to help us find out?

   Vary the kinds of light available to the plants using the filters while keeping everything else constant.

4. What do we think will happen? (hypothesis)

   Growing plants under different colors of light will result in observable differences in plant height, plant leaf size, or plant appearance.

5. What will we need to measure/observe?

   Height of the plants; sizes of the leaves; distances between adjacent stems; color of the plants could be observed; overall appearance of the plants could be observed.

An expected set of appropriate student responses might look like this:

Scientific Question: White light can be separated into light of many different colors. We know that plants need light to grow. What effect would the different colors of light individually have on plant growth?

Rationale/Hypothesis: We hypothesize that growing plants under different colors of light will affect their growth in ways that we can measure/observe.

Independent Variable (the variable that the experimenter varies): In this experiment, the independent variable is the color of light used.

Dependent Variable(s) (the variable(s) that vary in response to the experimentally-caused variation in the independent variable): Height and color of the treated plants.

Constants: Plant pot size, soil type, amount of soil, amount of water available, genetic constitution of the plants, size of the covering container.

Controls: Positive control: Plants grown in unfiltered light (if everything is working in the experiment, these should be normal).

Provision for Repeated Trials: Multiple seeds in each pot, multiple plants observed, and measured for all of the test and control pots.

References

Barrows, H.S. (1985). *How to design a problem-based curriculum for the preclinical years.* NY: Springer.

Bridges, E.M. (1992). *Problem-based learning for administrators.* Eugene, OR: ERIC Clearinghouse on Educational Management, University of Oregon. (ERIC Document Reproduction Service No. ED 347 617.)

Chickering, A.W., & Gamson, Z.F. (Eds.) (1991). *New directions for teaching and learning: No. 46. Applying the seven principles for good practice in undergraduate education.* San Francisco, CA: Jossey-Bass.

Joyce, B., & Weil, M. (1996). *Models of teaching* (5th ed.). Boston, MA: Allyn & Bacon.

Parnes, S.J. (1975). *Insights into creative behavior.* Buffalo, NY: DOK Publisher.

Suchman, J. (1964). *Studies in inquiry training.* In R. Ripple and V. Brookcastle (Eds.), Piaget reconsidered. (pp. 260–284). Ithaca, NY: Cornell University.

Treffinger, D.J. (in press). Creative problem solving: Overview and educational implications. *Educational Psychology Review.*

Treffinger, D.J., Isaksen, S.G., & Dorval, K.B. (1994). Creative problem solving: An overview. In M.A. Runco (Ed.), *Problem finding, problem solving, and creativity* (pp. 223–236). Norwood, NJ: Ablex Publishing Co.

Part IV

ASSESSING THE APPROPRIATENESS OF CURRICULUM FOR YOUR SCHOOL DISTRICT

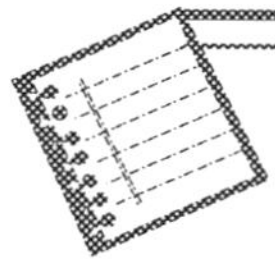

INTRODUCTION AND RATIONALE FOR SCIENCE CURRICULUM ASSESSMENT

The task of assessing science curricula for appropriateness becomes critical in the context of national reform in science education. Several national organizations such as the American Association for the Advancement of Science and the National Science Teachers' Association have called for all science education to make fundamental changes both in content and in presentation of material. Depth of conceptual understanding takes precedence over breadth of factual coverage in the recommendations in recognition of the rapidly expanding information base in science. All students should also be exposed to the nature of science, especially the practice of the scientific method and the attitudes of reasoned skepticism and tolerance of ambiguity associated with scientific thought. Changing the factual and didactic orientation of the current curricula and the materials that reinforce it to meet these new goals will require changing the very structures and foundations of the curriculum itself; a change in paradigm.

Two challenges are presented to reviewers of curricula who accept the validity and necessity of the "new science" model. The first is to find a way to rate current science curricula which is fair to the intent of the publishers and authors while attending to the assumption that in order to be effective, science instruction will follow a significantly new form. Basal texts which may be evaluated as perfectly sound under the old paradigm may in fact look less promising when rated using "new science" standards. Nevertheless, such a review provides part of the demonstration of where and how changes need to be made to meet the demands of the 21st century.

The second challenge is to find a new and appropriate set of standards for determining differentiation for high ability students. The AAAS report *Science for All Americans: A Project 2061 Report on Literary Goals in Science, Mathematics, and Technology* (1989) outlines scientific content, processes and attitudes which should be cultivated in all American students. This list, new to the goals of most general education programs, looks very much like the list of goals which teachers of the gifted have held for their students for some time. If all students should learn science concepts, learn to act and think like scientists, learn to independently hypothesize and experiment and analyze and infer, then what will the new set of standards for gifted students be?

A good core curriculum is an absolutely essential foundation to exemplary science instruction. Because of the interest in engaging students in science for the long term, it has become increasingly important to select or create science curriculum which simultaneously achieves several goals:

- The delivery of content which is substantive, up-to-date, and essential to an understanding of one or more science fields;
- The demonstration of science practices and "habits of mind" to give students practice in the behavior and thinking of scientists;
- The delivery of content and processes in a context which excites and entices students without diminishing the value of the content or reducing the practice of science to games or "magic"; and
- The opportunity for students to make connections between science areas and between science and other areas of study.

While such a core curriculum emphasis is essential for all learners, differentiating for the high ability learner requires responding to the scientific interests and behaviors displayed by these learners. These behaviors include early curiosity and understanding about the world of science; ability to master the tools of science by demonstrating the activities, beliefs, and characteristics of scientists; ability to reason analytically, deductively, and inductively with more complex material; and the energy and persistence to solve real problems of science. Thus, high ability learners need advanced science content earlier and at a more complex and abstract level than do other learners, even under the new science model.

The *Curriculum Assessment Guide to Science Materials* (CAG) establishes criteria and a review process for evaluating science curriculum for all learners. In addition, it identifies the features of science curriculum that are necessary to meet the needs of special populations of students. A subsequent publication, entitled *A Consumer's Guide to Science Curriculum* (Boyce, Johnson, Sher, Bailey, Gallagher, and VanTassel-Baska, 1993), illustrates the use of the *Curriculum Assessment Guide to Science Materials* by providing complete reviews of 27 sets of materials and a comparative analysis of the materials. Because curriculum materials are considered so crucial to the enterprise of science teaching, we believe that this set of criteria will prove valuable to school districts making materials decisions in science. The users of the guide may be 1) curriculum developers, 2) district-based curriculum or textbook review committees, or 3) individual teachers interested in materials for classroom use. We hope the process conveys a reasonable approach to decision-making about educational materials in science and that practitioners will find it helpful.

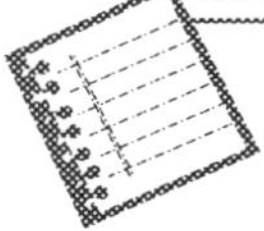

OVERVIEW OF THE REVIEW PROCESS

Our goals for curriculum review were: 1) to develop a comprehensive evaluation system that would provide a template for reviewing all science curriculum materials and 2) to generate curriculum reviews which would enable consumers to match available curricula with their local, identified needs. In order to reach these goals, we sought to conduct the following activities:

- To develop criteria by which a curriculum can be evaluated against a standard of excellence.
- To develop comprehensive criteria that would assess curricula in three areas: curriculum design, exemplary science, and tailoring for special populations.
- To create a system that would enable consumers to compare one set of materials to another.
- To provide a multifaceted review of curricula that couples a numerical rating system with the personal reactions and insights of the reviewers.
- To institute a collaborative review forum that incorporates the perspectives of a scientist, a curriculum development expert, and a materials specialist.

The review process illustrated in Figure I was designed as a collaborative endeavor that involved curriculum specialists, a scientist, and a materials specialist. The curriculum specialists' expertise included general curriculum development, specialized curriculum for gifted learners, and mathematics and technology. The scientist in the group had a specialty in molecular biology with research experience in university and pharmaceutical laboratories. The materials specialist had a background in library science and gifted education. The reviewers' classroom experience ranged from preschool to graduate school. In addition, each of them had experience teaching gifted learners at the elementary level and developing curriculum. This group with primary review responsibility was supported by a consultant group of educators and research scientists who provided information on current issues in science and state-of-the-art curriculum materials.

FIGURE I

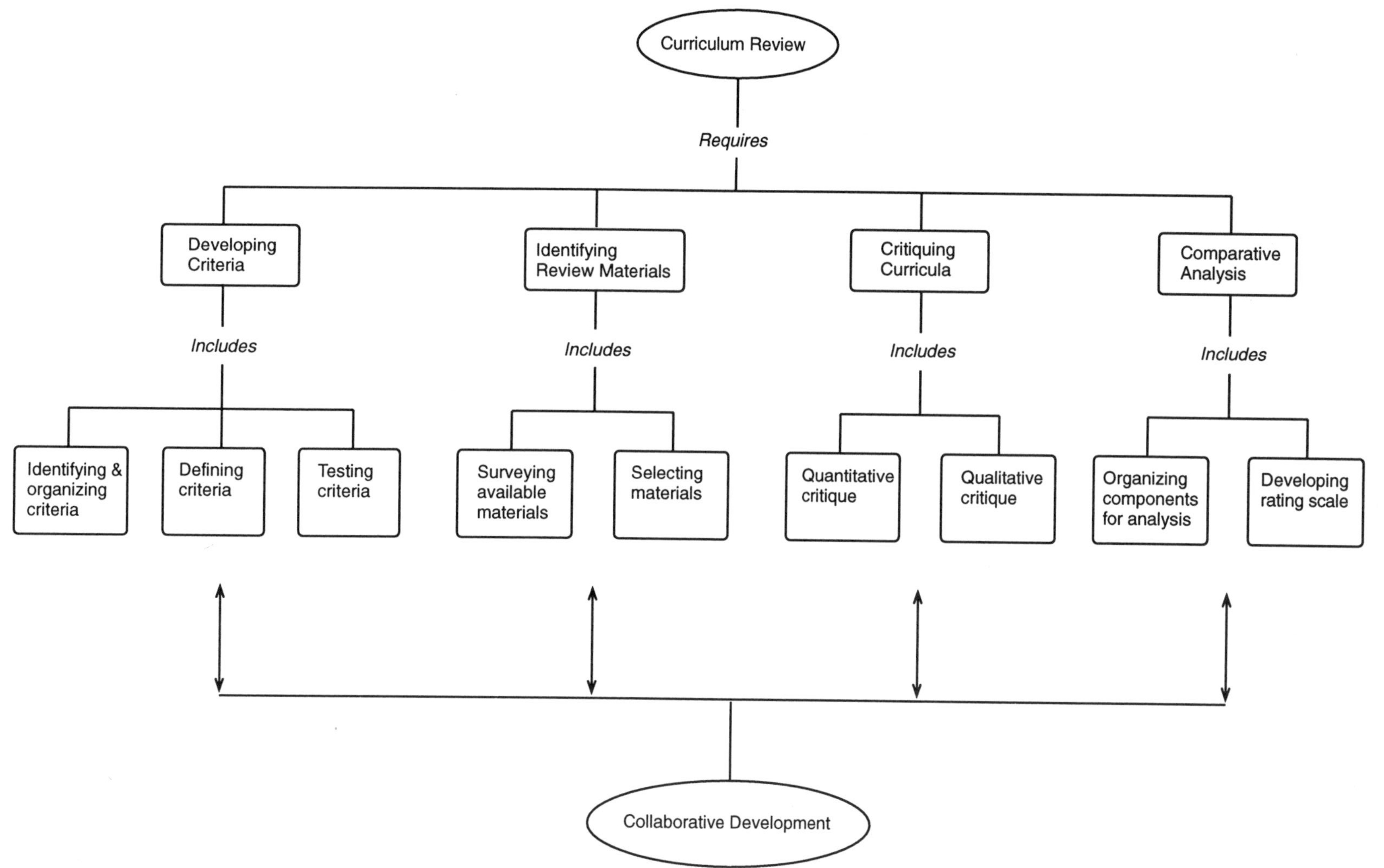

Curriculum Review
Requires
Developing Criteria
Identifying Review Materials
Critiquing Curricula
Comparative Analysis
Includes
Includes
Includes
Includes
Identifying & organizing criteria
Defining criteria
Testing criteria
Surveying available materials
Selecting materials
Quantitative critique
Qualitative critique
Organizing components for analysis
Developing rating scale
Collaborative Development

Developing criteria

The development of criteria was the cornerstone of the entire review process. The review team worked together to identify significant criteria, define each criterion, and test the criteria on sample curriculum. Identifying the criteria forced the team to consider the essential elements of curriculum which coalesced into three categories:

1. Curriculum features: elements that enable teachers to plan, deliver and assess instruction.
2. Exemplary science: elements of subject matter content and process.
3. Special populations: elements addressing the needs and concerns of particular student groups.

The work of VanTassel-Baska and her colleagues (VanTassel-Baska, 1992; VanTassel-Baska, Feldhusen, Seeley, Wheatley, Silverman, and Foster 1988) provided the foundational set of criteria for effective curriculum features and development. Specifically, this set looked at instructional objectives and how those objectives could be attained through the careful organization of activities, strategies and materials, and then assessed. The criteria addressed issues that ranged from "use of various types of questions" to "developmental readiness." Other sources that were used to develop criteria for curriculum design included the work of Krajcik and Berg (1987) and Walberg (1991).

The work of science organizations such as *Science for All Americans: Project 2061* (AAAS, 1989), *The National Science Teachers Association Handbooks I, III*, (Mechling and Oliver, 1983), and *Science Learning Matters* (NAEP, 1988) were reflected in the criteria for exemplary science instruction. The reports of these groups recommended that curricula integrate scientific thinking with scientific behaviors and attitudes, make inter- and intra-disciplinary connections, encourage active and real (not "cookbook") exploration, focus on learning key concepts instead of "covering the material," and demonstrate the connections between scientific discovery and moral and ethical decision-making. The criteria ensured that curricula provide students with the opportunity to study areas of science in which research is relatively new. From this kind of study, students learn the essential ambiguity of science, the role of personal values in interpreting data and that the study of science does not result in absolute answers.

The special populations for which specific criteria were developed included high ability learners, intellectually gifted and science prone students, girls, minority students, and disabled students. The work of VanTassel-Baska, et al. (1988) and Brandwein and Passow (1988) informed the criteria development for high ability learners as well as for intellectually gifted and science prone students. The criteria emphasized acceleration and compression of content, higher order thinking and scientific thinking skills, and the creation of real products. In order to engage girls and minorities in science, curriculum must be sensitive to their unique perspectives. For women, it means opportunities to "connect" information by representing it in a context which is personally relevant and to make associations among areas of study. For minorities, this means conscious adaptation of content to represent the perspectives of minority students and adaptation of instruction to fit their learning styles. For students with disabilities, it means providing greater individualization and flexibility in how, where, and under what circumstances science may be learned. Special population groups also benefit from the realization that science, far from being cold, impersonal and isolated, is intimately linked with the world of people. Criteria for the sections relating to girls, minority, and disabled students were based on the work of Eccles (1984), Hilton, Hsia, Solorzano, and Benton (1989), Laycock (1992), and Rosser (1986). Table I illustrates the focus of each criterial phase.

TABLE I
AN OVERVIEW OF ASSESSMENT PHASES AND CRITERIAL CATEGORIES

Criteria		
Phase I Curriculum Features	**Phase II Exemplary Science**	**Phase III Special Populations**
Curriculum Design	Content	High Ability
Classroom Design	Process	Science Prone
Technology		Minority Students
		Girls
		Disabled Students

After the criteria were identified, the review team worked together to define terms. At the onset, the group anticipated the need to translate the technical languages of science and education for one another. However, they were less prepared for the more complex cultural issues of educators and scientists learning to work together. To educators, for instance, "scientific method" involves the three steps of generating a hypothesis, testing the hypothesis, and reaching a logical conclusion. To scientists, the "scientific process" represents a recursive mode of thinking, investigating, and communicating (Sher, 1992). Over time, differences of perspective came to be seen as informing insights rather than conflicting standards. These insights were then reflected in the descriptors of each criterion, and they informed the entire review process.

Finally, the team tested the criteria by applying them to various curricula and comparing each team member's ratings. The tests and ensuing discussions led to new definitions and to revisions of criteria. In addition, team members located superior and inferior examples of various criteria; these examples then served as benchmarks for evaluating other curricula.

IDENTIFYING MATERIALS FOR REVIEW

The second stage of the review process, identifying materials for review, included surveying available science curricula and then selecting the curricula which would be reviewed. As a first step in the survey, project consultants presented an overview of science curriculum from the 1960's to the present. Secondly, the National Science Resources Center (NSRC), a curriculum resource center and information database established by the Smithsonian Institution and the National Academy of Sciences, served as a major source of information. As well as providing specific information about science curricula, the NSRC publications, *Science for Children: Resources for Teachers* (1988) and the *NSRC Newsletter* (1988–to date) provided the names and addresses of science curriculum publishers and producers. Letters soliciting curriculum for review were sent to all of the sources listed in the NSRC publications. Finally, a literature search that included the ERIC CD-ROM database and current professional science and science education journals was conducted to access new materials. The survey of science curricula resulted in a working, annotated bibliography that listed 62 sets of materials.

From the working bibliography, 27 sets of curriculum materials were selected for review. The rationale for selecting the materials included:

- breadth of use,
- evidence of appropriateness for high ability learners, and
- innovations or prototypical materials of new science components.

These materials were then critiqued using both quantitative and qualitative approaches. For a full treatment of this process see Johnson, Boyce, and VanTassel-Baska (1995).

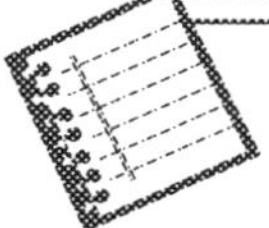

WHY SCHOOLS NEED TO REVIEW SCIENCE MATERIALS

The implications of the review component of this project go beyond the method for reviewing curriculum materials and the evaluative information published in this guide. In order for educators at all levels of instruction to make informed decisions about instruction, they must first become informed consumers. The model described here offers a way to examine current practices embedded in the materials we use in classrooms and to initiate change that is necessary for instructional improvement and educational reform.

THE REVIEW PROCESS ENHANCES DECISION MAKING

A collaborative review process is useful at all levels of instruction. At the classroom level, it enables teachers to make informed choices by providing the criteria to choose challenging materials for valid, worthy activities and the knowledge base to dismiss time-consuming distractions. For instance, the "interdisciplinary art activity" encountered in one respected set of materials which asks students to construct an igloo out of sugar cubes during the study of temperature and insulation will be rejected for lacking content and valid experience in both science and art. Likewise, didactic materials with worthy but simplistic messages such as "save the environment" will be rejected for the more accurate and thought-provoking materials that consider the various sides of complex scientific issues.

At the school level, the collaborative review process provides principals and librarians with a vehicle for involving the entire staff in decision-making on materials acquisitions. At the system and state level, it adds rigor to the textbook adoption process. The process provides an in-depth, systematic way to compare one curriculum with another, and it illuminates the lack of research base for many of the heavily marketed, commercial curricula.

THE REVIEW PROCESS FACILITATES COLLABORATION

The process of collaborative curriculum review offers an ongoing model to examine what's working and what's not working for curriculum delivery within a local school or within a school system. Once a set of criteria become understood by a group and internalized, teachers and administrators have a method by which to improve instruction. In addition to defining terms and agreeing on standards, the process includes seeing another's perspective and tapping into another realm of expertise.

The expertise within buildings, systems, and communities becomes available for meaningful, productive collaboration. Classroom teachers, subject specialists or experts in other fields, educators of special populations such as gifted learners and at-risk groups, guidance counselors and psychologists, librarians and media specialists all contribute different but essential knowledge and perspective. Collaborative review becomes a self-generating, learning process that results not just in a curriculum review but a heightened awareness of possibilities for effective classroom practice.

The review process is dynamic

To be effective and viable, the review process and model require constant revisiting. For example, new research on the learning process and the consideration of evolving technology must continue to be incorporated into the criteria. In essence, continually revising criteria is part of an informed consumer process and essential to intellectual life. It is a fundamental aspect of education and one that teachers need to impart to students.

One of the values of this review process is that it considers curriculum resources other than textbooks. Tulley and Farr (1990) argue, "As long as educators continue to assume that the textbook is the curriculum, teachers will be powerless to exert change" (p. 169). The review process makes it evident that alternative materials such as modular curricula combine content and process in more powerful ways than reading-based textbooks. The need for change becomes urgently clear when choices are seen in a broader context, thereby expanding the range of possibilities.

Instructional improvement and the restructuring of schools depends on a shared vision of various groups and disciplines. Collaborative review offers a way for groups to identify mutual goals, to determine the criteria for excellence, and to work together. The implications of this review process for effective collaboration combined with the possibilities for staff development and instructional improvement warrant serious consideration.

Definitions of Criteria for Review

In the following section, the list of relevant criteria to consider in reviewing science curriculum materials is provided for all three phases of consideration. Each criterion is accompanied by a definition.

General Curriculum Features Evaluation Form (Phase I Review)

Curriculum Design

1. ***Rationale and Purpose***

   This feature addresses the reasons for developing a particular unit of study for use with a given group of learners at a particular stage of development. It provides the reader with a sense of the importance of the topic under study and why it is being taught.

   —substantive and worthy?

   Content is important and valuable; publishers/authors provide reasons why content was selected or the value is self-evident.

   —clear and understandable?

   Teachers can easily tell why the selected content is important. Rationale and purpose are written in meaningful and clear language rather than in educational and/or scientific jargon.

   —logical order and integrated structure to scope and sequence?

   The suggested order for presentation of topics and concepts makes sense both within a grade and from grade to grade.

   —identified outcomes consonant with purpose?

   The content and processes identified as desired goals of learning are consistent with the stated reasons to learn.

2. ***Curriculum Content***

   This feature provides the scope of the unit in respect to content treatment and allows the reader to see the interrelationships of ideas that will guide the unit development process.

   —significant scientific concepts?

   The science content is central to fundamental understanding about a science content area and/or the scientific process.

   —significant information to explore concepts in depth?

   Enough factual information should be provided to cover selected concepts in depth, as opposed to a cursory sampling of information across many concepts.

   —topics support concepts?

   Individual areas of study in the curriculum illuminate/provide examples for larger, more abstract science concepts.

   —engaging style of present information?

   The material is attractive (well-illustrated, up-to-date, etc.), catches the attention of the learner, and engages the learner.

   —topics and activities have personal meaning and social relevance for students?

   Information is presented from a child's point of reference.

   —allowance for curricular differentiation for gifted learners?

   The possibility to adjust content level or pace and acceleration of the curriculum exists. Suggestions for such adaptations are provided.

3. *Curriculum Responsiveness to Developmental Needs*

This feature of the curriculum assures that there is an optimal match between the developmental readiness of the learner and the curricular expectations.

—sequential exposure to scientific concepts from the concrete to the abstract?

Depending on the age and/or grade level, the science ideas shift from being tangible with hands-on tasks and/or basic explanations to a more abstract and generalizable form.

—manipulative science materials used to support the curriculum?

There are activities and resources available or suggested so that students can "do" science.

—high active to passive activity ratio?

The curriculum requires that students be active through numerous hands-on activities.

—sequential use of visual materials from the picto-centric to the text-centered?

Content is presented primarily through engaging and interesting pictures in early primary grades and moves to proportionately higher percentage of written text in higher grades.

—materials challenge students' current explanations and allow time for them to reconstruct their understanding of scientific phenomena?

Since students often hold primitive or incorrect views of scientific phenomena, the materials force them to recognize their own incorrect ideas and re-evaluate their thinking.

Classroom Design

4. *Instructional Objectives*

This feature provides the focus and direction for learning in the unit. It specifies anticipated outcomes for students as a result of being taught a unit of study.

—clear and understandable?

A curriculum reader would know immediately what the students will be able to know and/or do as a result of a unit of study.

—measurable?

Techniques or suggestions are provided for teachers so they can tell whether or not they have achieved the learning outcomes.

—related to overall rationale and purpose?

The goals of an individual unit are consistent with the goals of the curriculum as a whole.

5. *Activities*

This feature specifies what teachers will do to facilitate learning and what students will do to learn.

—appropriate balance of teacher direction/student direction?

Room is provided in the curriculum both to meet teacher goals and to allow for students to participate and contribute to the class.

—developmentally appropriate activities?

The activities take into account the level of cognitive, emotional and physical development that is likely to be found in learners who will be doing these activities. Activities are challenging, yet achievable.

—activities used to introduce topic (get students to explore topic to be studied)?

The activities used to get students interested in the topics are fun/interesting, rather than reading or lecture.

—activities clarify, reinforce and extend content?

Activities serve a purpose related to learning content beyond repeating what students already know. They directly support the content-base of the unit.

—science integrated with other subjects, specifically language arts and mathematics?

Interdisciplinary connections are presented.

6. *Instructional Strategies*

This feature provides direction to readers around the major approaches to teaching that will be undertaken. It specifies heuristic models, questioning techniques, and conferencing approaches used by the teacher.

—are strategies varied?

Several different forms of instruction are suggested (e.g. inquiry activities, lecture, laboratory work, independent work, etc.)

—opportunities for problem finding and solving?

Students are encouraged to identify and solve problems that are not explicitly set out for them in advance.

—opportunities for open inquiry?

Problems, projects, etc. are open-ended with respect to the solution or approach to the solution. Students are encouraged to formulate questions and explore possible answers to those questions.

—varied grouping approach, e.g., including opportunities for small group work?

The curriculum suggests both large and small group activities and different ways these groups can be formed and used.

—cooperative work focuses on real problems with problem resolution rather than problem solution as goal?

The process of solving problems is treated as more important than the "right answer."

—opportunities to practice decision making strategies?

Students are encouraged to make decisions rather than have the teachers tell them all procedures and outcomes.

—use of various types of questions (e.g., convergent, divergent, evaluative)?

There are a variety of questions suggested which stimulate different levels of thought, from knowledge through evaluation.

7. *Assessment Procedures*

This feature specifies how students will be assessed in respect to their learning in the unit. It provides documentation for learning outcomes.

—presence of pre/post assessment measures?

There are opportunities at both the beginning and the end of the unit to measure knowledge so that relative gain can be measured.

—use of observational evaluation?

Opportunities for assessment by observation are included.

—use of authentic assessment?

There are opportunities to evaluate students doing "real," actual science rather than a written test.

—objective attainment assessment measures?

There are evaluation strategies which measure directly whether or not the student has met an objective.

—assessment based on ability to get and to use information?

Assessment procedures require students to access and use information, rather than simply recognize facts.

—assessment based on outcomes of significance?

The objectives that are assessed are ones that are valuable and important to science concepts, processes, or attitudes.

—opportunity for overall evaluation?

Opportunity is provided for a holistic, integrated final evaluation. There is some way of assessing whether objectives for whole unit or curriculum have been achieved.

8. *Materials/Resources*

This feature provides bibliographic references for use in implementing the unit. It includes both resources for teachers and materials for student use.

—instructional materials begin with students' current knowledge?

The materials provide for diagnostic assessment of knowledge and skills and/or introductory activities that encourage teacher assessment of knowledge levels.

—supportive bibliography for teachers?

Resources are suggested for teachers to enhance their knowledge of the subject.

—frequent student misconceptions are identified for teachers?

Teachers are alerted to what errors or pitfalls students commonly make or experience.

—bibliography for student extension reading?

Bibliographies are provided for the learners.

—supportive handout materials (informational, worksheets, etc.)?

Materials are included that are ready for duplication and that support the basic curriculum unit.

9. *Extension Ideas*

This feature specifies follow-up learning opportunities for students that go beyond the prepared unit of study but are logical next activities, based on unit work. Suggestions for both group and independent work should be encouraged.

—worthwhile, related activities for students to pursue independently?

Meaningful suggestions are included for ways a student can extend the school learning experience to the home environment. Ideas, activities, and resources are suggested so the individual student can do extended work on a given topic, concept or theme.

Technology Features*

This set of features specifies the extent to which the technology aspect of the curriculum is appropriate and effective in enhancing science learning experiences.

General

—actively engages students in higher order thinking skills and activities?
—enhances and complements instruction?
—provides effective interaction?
—allows exploration otherwise prohibited by time, danger, or money?
—provides simulations of models or experiments that cannot be experienced with real materials?
—contains several levels of difficulty?
—provides useful, corrective feedback?
—easy to use?

Technical

—uncluttered screen design?
—lucid, economical text?
—dynamic visuals for abstract concepts?
—useful help screens?
—effective self-pacing devices?
—comprehensive teacher manual that includes instructions for use and modification, inventory, and specifications?

*These features may not be evident.

Definitions of Criteria
Exemplary Science Features Evaluation Form
(Phase II Review)

Science Content

1. —content base in key areas of science that provide the fundamentals of basic science?

   The curriculum covers areas of science that are basic for a good understanding of modern science, rather than covering trivial or peripheral topics.

2. —content base in key areas of technology?

   The curriculum covers areas that are basic for an understanding of modern technology, rather than showcasing flashy or otherwise inaccessible technology.

3. —inclusion of current science/technology content?

   The scientific content is up-to-date; discoveries made in the last decade which are germane to the material are discussed; content reflects an understanding of current science by the curriculum writers.

4. —inclusion of historical and current science/technology issues?

   Historic and current science/technology issues (such as AIDS or the catastrophe theory of the extinction of the dinosaurs) are included to give students a sense of the controversy which can accompany the introduction of new scientific ideas.

5. —topics linked to broad scientific concepts (intradisciplinary connections)?

   The topics covered are explained in terms of their relevance to broad scientific concepts (such as evolution) rather than presented as unconnected facts or ideas.

6. —topics linked to ideas outside of science (interdisciplinary connections)?

   Scientific topics of immediate relevance to areas outside science are discussed and explicitly linked to those areas.

7. —balance of qualitative and quantitative information?

   Scientific information is presented in both narrative and numerical terms as appropriate. The curriculum does not shy away from necessary quantitative information.

8. —balance of theoretical and practical science?

   Both the theories of science (gravity and the Copernican theory) and their applications (eclipse, prediction, seasons, artificial satellites) are presented.

9. —presence of moral and ethical dimensions of science and technology?

   Science and technology should be presented as initiating new, complex and ambiguous moral and ethical dilemmas which require discussion and resolution by parties with conflicting viewpoints.

10. —global perspectives on relationship of science and technology to society and to developing nations?

    Science and technology should be presented as a part of the real world; their effects on and implications for society should be discussed.

11. —science is accurate and presented understandably?

    The science presented is factually correct and presented such that the important facts and ideas of the area under discussion are readily apparent.

12. —important science concepts are covered in depth?

The curriculum presents sufficient information on the important ideas of science for the student to be able to understand their power and relevance. Trivial and inessential material does not compete with important material for the student's attention.

Science Process

13. —provision for the use of technology (e.g., computers, CD-ROM) as it can be applied to science?

The curriculum provides for the use of appropriate technology by students for their own scientific purposes (not merely for science TEACHING purposes).

14. —opportunities for open-ended scientific investigation (not simply verification exercises)?

Opportunities for scientific investigation in which the student may not know the answer or have a protocol provided beforehand are present; students can design and perform their own experiments.

15. —use of community resources?

Suggestions are made when appropriate for use of community resources. Examples would include "take a field trip to see . . . ," "bring in a nurse to talk about . . .," and so on.

16. —laboratory and field-work integral to and integrated with the curriculum?

Any use of the curriculum demands that the students actively participate in labs and fieldwork. Labs are not optional activities, but rather contribute directly to the development of the child's scientific understanding.

17. —opportunities for students to have personal interaction with people practicing science?

Suggestions are made for the integration of scientists into the students' science experience. For example, the strong suggestions could be made that a doctor be brought in to discuss nutrition, rather than the teacher; that a geologist be brought along on a field trip; and so on.

18. —concern for career awareness?

Students are exposed to the various jobs associated with a given field of science.

19. —opportunities for students to work together to investigate a scientific/technological problem?

Students should be given the opportunity to investigate a scientific problem by working cooperatively in small groups.

20. —opportunities for students to work with a mentor to investigate a scientific/technological problem?

Students should be given the opportunity to investigate a science problem under the guidance of an adult mentor.

21. —use of various questioning strategies integrated throughout the curriculum?

Students should be challenged through the use of higher level (evaluation, synthesis, and analysis) questions and be asked to think thoroughly with the use of probing questions.

22. —active student involvement required by curriculum?

Students cannot "get by" by reading the book and listening in class. They must also participate in laboratory activities, contribute to discussions, write reports, and investigate scientific problems alone or in groups.

23. —scientific process demonstrated as approximation versus absolute rigidity?

    Students must be given an understanding of the way scientific ideas are developed (educated hunches, inference, and speculation supported by experiments with limitations), both by curriculum containing descriptions of scientific controversies and their resolution and by actively doing science in the lab and field.

24. —students are taught to build and test hypotheses?

    Students should be required to design and perform experiments, building hypotheses using their understanding of science and the world and then testing them experimentally.

25. —allowance for questioning of assumptions and diverse opinions?

    Opportunities should be present for students to experience the development of a scientific idea; different points of view, questioning of the viewpoints and assumptions of others, and the acquisition and presentation of additional information to resolve disputed points should be included.

26. —examples of unsuccessful science so that science-as-a-process is demonstrated?

    Students should be allowed both to obtain negative or ambiguous experimental results and to read about scientists who had similar experiences in the lab. This is most likely to happen in open-ended experimental situations.

Definitions of Criteria
Tailoring for Special Populations Evaluation Form (Phase III Review)

Differentiation for High Ability Learners

1. —provisions for acceleration and compression of content?

   Curriculum skills and concepts are organized on a sequence from "easy to difficult" concepts that would allow for easy teacher adaptation to students' individual instructional level.

2. —use of higher order thinking skills?

   The curriculum includes activities and questions that require learners to think at the levels of analysis, synthesis, and evaluation.

3. —integration of content by key ideas, issues, and themes?

   The curriculum is organized according to broad-based concepts in science, such as change, patterns, and systems.

4. —connection of scientific ideas to other disciplines?

   The curriculum illustrates how scientific ideas have salience in other content areas such as music, art, literature, social science, and mathematics.

5. —opportunities for both inductive and deductive reasoning?

   The curriculum guides students 1) to create specific illustrations, examples, and details that support a given generalization, and 2) to engage in thinking to form generalizations from specific case examples or data that are provided.

6. —use of multiple teaching resources?

   The curriculum encourages the use of multiple media, multiple readings, and multiple activities from other materials to teach skills and concepts.

7. —use of diagnostic-prescriptive teaching?

   The curriculum provides an assessment approach that allows for pre-testing and post-testing as well as on-going assessment of learners' mastery of skills and concepts.

8. —attention to instructional pacing?

   The teachers' guide notes that some learners can master the basic science content at a rate faster than other learners.

9. —advanced reading level?

   The curriculum readability index is pitched at least one or two grade levels beyond the given designated level.

10. —opportunities for students to develop advanced products?

    The curriculum provides suggestions for teachers to support student projects that involve original investigation.

11. —opportunities for independent learning based on student capacity and interest?

    The curriculum provides extension activities to be undertaken by students alone in various settings.

12. —use of inquiry-based instructional techniques?

    The curriculum is based on a model of questioning that promotes the role of the student as investigator.

Curriculum Responsiveness to Intellectually Gifted

The materials provide consideration for the top five percent of the student population through the sufficiently advanced content, complex applications of concepts, and appropriately designed product demands.

Curriculum Responsiveness to Science Prone Students

The materials provide consideration for students who have an avid interest in and aptitude for doing science through immersion on open-ended exploration, in-depth independent work, and opportunities to work with a mentor.

Curriculum Responsiveness to Girls

The materials provide consideration for gender bias and stereotyping, use of positive role models, and inclusion of teaching strategies found conducive to girls' enhanced learning.

Curriculum Responsiveness to Minority Concerns

The materials provide consideration for ethnic bias and stereotyping, use of positive role models, inclusion of non-Western cultural contributions to science, and strategies found conducive to minority students enhanced learning.

Curriculum Responsiveness to Disabled Students

The materials provide consideration for broad individual differences through individualized techniques and practices, tools for compensation, and attention to varied formats for guided practice.

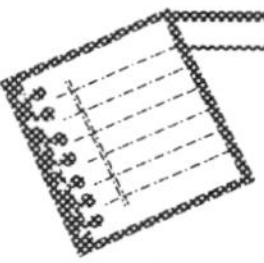

PROCEDURES FOR USING THE CAG FORMS

1. Select a review team composed of teachers, administrators, and specialists with expertise in general curriculum, science curriculum, and curriculum for high ability learners. Remember to include your library media specialist as a part of this group. A review team model should not exceed 6–8 individuals.
2. Read and review the CAG as a group, especially the review forms and the underlying definitions for the criteria presented in them.
3. Collect materials for team review.
4. Assign your most experienced reviewers to rate all three phases (no more than two individuals). Then assign each of the remaining reviewers the phase that corresponds best to their expertise. At least two reviews should be done for each individual phase.
5. Use the accompanying review forms for this process.
6. Compile data across reviewers on the overall rating form and hold a team session to discuss reviews according to the specific material reviewed.
7. Make materials selection decisions based on a) the match between the materials and the goals and objectives of your district science program, b) the match with district needs for supplementary materials, and c) the match with special population needs.

CURRICULUM ASSESSMENT GUIDE OVERALL RATING

The Curriculum Assessment Guide Overall Rating Form found on the next page provides a model for synthesizing the key features evaluated for each set of curriculum materials reviewed. The numerical average of reviewed ratings for each feature may be transferred onto this single sheet so that rating recommendations might be made according to individual features of the curriculum. For example, some curricula may be very strong in science and thus recommended for that feature. The same curricula may be found inadequate in general curriculum features and thus not recommended based on that set of criteria. The purpose and function of this rating form, then, is to provide a shorthand coding for the results of the multi-layered review process.

THE CURRICULUM ASSESSMENT GUIDE OVERALL RATING FORM

	Phase I: General Curriculum Features	**Phase II: Exemplary Science Features**	**Phase III: Tailoring for Special Populations**	**Notes**
Reviewer #1				
Reviewer #2				
Reviewer #3				
Reviewer #4				
Reviewer #5				
Reviewer #6				
Reviewer #7				
Reviewer #8				

Notes: Appropriate for (A) Intellectually Gifted; (B) Science Prone; (C) Girls; (D) Minorities; (E) Disabled Students

THE CURRICULUM ASSESSMENT FORMS

GENERAL CURRICULUM FEATURES
PHASE I

Name of Reviewer: ______________________________

Title: ______________________________

Title of Curriculum to be Reviewed: ______________________________

Appropriate Grade Level(s): ____________ Original Copyright Date: ____________

Date(s) of Revision: ______________

Directions: Carefully read through all curriculum materials and then rate the curriculum by each of the following criteria on a scale of: 5 = To an exemplary extent; 4 = To a good extent; 3 = Adequate; 2 = To a limited extent; and 1 = Not at all.

1. *Rationale and Purpose*					
—substantive and worthy?	5	4	3	2	1
—clear and understandable?	5	4	3	2	1
—order of topics and concepts makes sense within and across grades?	5	4	3	2	1
2. *Instructional Objectives*					
—clear and understandable?	5	4	3	2	1
—measurable?	5	4	3	2	1
—related to overall rationale and purpose?	5	4	3	2	1
3. *Activities*					
—appropriate balance of teacher direction/student direction?	5	4	3	2	1
—developmentally appropriate activities?	5	4	3	2	1
—activities clarify, reinforce and extend content?	5	4	3	2	1
—numerous hands-on activities?	5	4	3	2	1
4. *Instructional Strategies*					
—varied strategies (e.g., inquiry activities, lecture, laboratory work, independent work)?	5	4	3	2	1
—opportunities for open inquiry that include problem finding, problem solving, and decision making?	5	4	3	2	1
—varied grouping approaches including opportunities for small group and independent work?	5	4	3	2	1
—use of various types of questions (e.g., convergent, divergent, evaluative)?	5	4	3	2	1
—worthwhile, related extension activities are included?	5	4	3	2	1

5. *Assessment Procedures*

—presence of pre/post assessment measures?	5	4	3	2	1
—use of authentic assessment that measures attainment of the objectives?	5	4	3	2	1
—criteria for student assessment are stated?	5	4	3	2	1
—assessment based on student ability to get and to use information?	5	4	3	2	1

6. *Materials/Resources*

—engaging style of presenting information?	5	4	3	2	1
—background material for teachers such as explanation of concepts and identification of students' common misconceptions?	5	4	3	2	1
—bibliographies for teacher support and student extension?	5	4	3	2	1
—supportive handout materials (informational worksheets, etc)?	5	4	3	2	1

7. *Technology (if applicable)*

—actively engages students in higher order thinking skills and activities?	5	4	3	2	1
—enhances and complements instruction?	5	4	3	2	1
—provides simulations of models or experiments that cannot be experienced with real materials?	5	4	3	2	1

Overall average score for Phase I review: ☐

Comments on strengths/weaknesses:

EXEMPLARY SCIENCE FEATURES
PHASE II

Name of Reviewer: ______________________________

Title: ______________________________

Title of Curriculum to be Reviewed: ______________________________

Appropriate Grade Level(s): __________ Original Copyright Date: __________

Date(s) of Revision: __________

Directions: Carefully read through all curriculum materials and then rate the curriculum by each of the following criteria on a scale of: 5 = To an exemplary extent; 4 = To a good extent; 3 = Adequate; 2 = To a limited extent, and 1 = Not at all.

Science Content

1. —important science concepts are covered in-depth?	5	4	3	2	1
2. —science is accurate and presented understandably?	5	4	3	2	1
3. —topics linked to broad scientific concepts (intradisciplinary connections)?	5	4	3	2	1
4. —topics linked to ideas outside of science (interdisciplinary connections)?	5	4	3	2	1
5. —balance of qualitative and quantitative information?	5	4	3	2	1
6. —balance of theoretical and practical science?	5	4	3	2	1
7. —presence of moral, ethical, and historical dimensions of science and technology?	5	4	3	2	1

Science Process

8. —opportunities for open-ended scientific investigation (not simply verification exercises)?	5	4	3	2	1
9. —laboratory and field work integral to and integrated with the curriculum?	5	4	3	2	1
10. —opportunities for students to work together to investigate a real-world scientific technological problem?	5	4	3	2	1
11. —students are taught to build and test hypotheses?	5	4	3	2	1
12. —allowance for questioning of assumptions and diverse opinions?	5	4	3	2	1

Overall average score for Phase II review: [ ]

Comments on strengths/weaknesses:

TAILORING FOR SPECIAL POPULATIONS
PHASE III

Name of Reviewer: ______________________________

Title: ______________________________

Title of Curriculum to be Reviewed: ______________________________

Appropriate Grade Level(s): ______________________________

Although curriculum may be found exemplary from a technical and even subject area perspective, it is important to consider the extent to which curriculum can be tailored to the needs of more targeted groups of learners with special needs. Thus the Phase III review process looks more closely at the features of exemplary curriculum for special populations.

Directions: Carefully re-read through all curriculum materials and then, rate the curriculum by each of the following criteria on a scale of: 5 = To an exemplary extent; 4 = To a good extent; 3 = Adequate; 2 = To a limited extent; and 1 = Not at all.

Differentiation for High Ability Learners

1. —provisions for acceleration and compression of content?	5	4	3	2	1
2. —use of higher order thinking skills (e. g., analysis, synthesis, evaluation)?	5	4	3	2	1
3. —integration of content by key ideas, issues, and themes?	5	4	3	2	1
4. —advanced reading level?	5	4	3	2	1
5. —opportunities for students to develop advanced products?	5	4	3	2	1
6. —opportunities for independent learning based on student capacity and interest?	5	4	3	2	1
7. —use of inquiry-based instructional techniques?	5	4	3	2	1

Overall average score for Phase III review: [ ]

Comments on strengths/weaknesses:

A. Curriculum Responsiveness to the Intellectually Gifted 5 4 3 2 1

—sufficiently advanced in content?
—complex applications of concepts?
—product demands appropriately designed?

B. Curriculum Responsiveness to the Science Prone 5 4 3 2 1

—opportunities for in-depth, independent work on selected topics?
—immersion in open-ended exploration?
—opportunities to work with a mentor?

C. Curriculum Responsiveness to Girls 5 4 3 2 1

—presence of information about contribution of women to science?
—opportunities to read about women in science?
—avoidance of bias and sex stereotyping in resource materials and career information?
—use of varied teaching strategies, indcluding hands-on, discussion, and cooperative learning?
—use of conceptual organizers for teaching new material?

D. Curriculum Responsiveness to Minority Concerns 5 4 3 2 1

—incorporation of effective social experiences?
—global perspective with attention to non-Western cultures?
—emphasis on analogical reasoning and associative thinking?
—presence of information about contribution for minorities to science?
—avoidance of bias and ethnic stereotyping in resource materials and career information?

E. Curriculum Responsiveness to Disabled Students 5 4 3 2 1

—options for individualized programming?
—opportunities for variety of response modes?
—provision of tools for compensation?
—use of varied formats for guided and independent practice?

Special populations for which materials are appropriate:
(Circle all that apply.)

A	B	C	D	E

Comments on strengths/weaknesses:

References

American Association for the Advancement of Science. (1989). *Science for all Americans: A project 2061 report on literacy goals in science, mathematics, and technology*. Washington, DC: Author.

Boyce, L.N., Johnson, D.T., Sher, B.T., Bailey, J.M., Gallagher, S.A., VanTassel-Baska, J. (1993). *A consumer's guide to science curriculum*. Williamsburg, VA: College of William and Mary, Center for Gifted Education.

Brandwein, P.F. & Passow, A. (Eds.). (1988). *Gifted young in science: Potential through performance*. Washington, DC: National Science Teachers Association.

Eccles, J. (1984). Sex differences in mathematics participation. In M. Steinkamp and M.L. Maehr (Eds.), *Women in science*. Greenwich, CT: J.A.I. Press.

Hilton, T.L., Hsia, J., Solorzano, D.G., & Benton, N.L. (1989). *Persistence in science of high-ability minority students*. Princeton, NJ: Educational Testing Service.

Johnson, D., Boyce, L.N., & VanTassel-Baska, J. (1995). Evaluating curriculum materials in science. *Gifted Child Quarterly, 89* (1), 35–43.

Krajcik, J.S. & Berg, C. (1987). Exemplary software for the science classroom. *School Science and Mathematics*, *87*, 494–500.

Laycock, V. (1992). Curricula for exceptional children: A special education perspective in J. VanTassel-Baska. *Planning Effective Curriculum for Gifted Learners*. (pp. 243–260). Denver, CO: Love Publishing.

Mechling, K.R., & Oliver, D.L. (1983). *Handbook I: Science teaches basic skills; Handbook III: Characteristics of a good elementary science program; Handbook IV: What research says about elementary school science*. Washington, DC: National Science Teachers Association.

National Assessment of Educational Progress (1988). *Science learning matters*. Princeton, NJ: Educational Testing Service.

National Science Resource Center. (1988). *Science for children: resources or teachers*. Washington, DC: National Academy Press.

NSRC Newsletter. (1988–to date). Washington, DC: Smithsonian Institution, National Science Resources Center.

Rosser, S.V. (1986). *Teaching science and health from a feminist perspective*. NY: Pergamon.

Sher, B.T. (1992). *Guide to science concepts*. Williamsburg, VA: College of William and Mary, Center for Gifted Education.

Tulley, M. & Farr, R. (1990). Textbook evaluation and selection. In D.L. Elliott and A. Woodward (Eds.), *Textbooks and Schooling in the United States: Eighty-ninth Yearbook of the National Society for the Study of Education, Part I* (pp. 162–177). Chicago, IL: University of Chicago Press.

VanTassel-Baska, J. (1992). *Planning effective curriculum for gifted learners*. Denver, CO: Love Publishing.

VanTassel-Baska, J., Feldhusen, J., Seeley, K., Wheatley, G., Silverman, L., & Foster, W. (1988). *Comprehensive curriculum for gifted learners*. Boston, MA: Allyn & Bacon.

Walberg, H.J. (1991). *Improving school science in advanced and developing countries*. Review of Educational Research, 61, 25–69.

Part V

SUPPORT STRUCTURES FOR SUCCESSFUL IMPLEMENTATION

Support Structures for Successful Implementation

In each of the concluding sessions of summer institutes held at the College of William and Mary over three years, we asked participants what they saw as some of the major issues or obstacles facing them in implementing the William and Mary problem-based science units.

Those issues or concerns basically fell into the following categories:

- *Support: administrators, other teachers, parents*
- *Resources: time, people, materials, money, space*
- *Staff development: personal, school and district wide, team building, articulation with other levels*
- *The change process and the retreat to the "comfort zone"*

These issues primarily focused on getting the support of other educators at the school and/or district level so as to make both the investment of personal effort and time as well as the search for resources and training focused and profitable. They came from the realization that curricular change, for long term success, needs to be a system-wide process rather than simply a single teacher or team going it alone.

Some Special Issues

Personal Knowledge: An immediate and serious concern discussed by some participants focused on the fact that they would need to learn more "real" science and critical thinking skills before attempting specific units. This is an honest need as these units do include advanced, high level content. Certainly we recommend that teachers become very familiar with the material well in advance of starting the unit, whether it be during the summer or the school year. However, we also strongly recommend sharing the load through various approaches to teaming.

One way of providing additional expertise is, of course, to locate experts in the community who might be able to act as mentors to the class or to individual students. Secondary level science teachers should also be able to provide some specialized knowledge and skills. Bringing them into the problem-based learning process may also allay their fears that you are usurping "their content." Including secondary level teachers will also allow for and encourage better articulation between levels and subjects.

Finally, always consider the use of other students, secondary or university level, as content experts. They can help demonstrate that elementary students can handle high level scientific concepts. The science units are multidisciplinary and therefore experts can also come from outside the realm of science, in such areas as social studies, math, and language arts.

Appropriate Facilities: Along with personal knowledge of subject is the need for appropriate facilities in which to operate in the PBL mode. An up-to-date science room would be ideal for conducting these activities; however, it is not mandatory and lack of it should not necessarily prevent one from implementing the units. Running water, tables, counter space, storage space, good ventilation, etc. are sufficient for most of the activities found within the units. Access to computers, telephones and libraries for both teacher and students is important. Also some of the activities require undisturbed long-term space which may pose a problem in some schools. All students must be reminded of the safety issues inherent in dealing with real-life problems and the teacher must assess the space for appropriateness prior to initiation of any unit.

Textbooks: Another common concern mentioned by institute participants was the use of textbooks. Since these science units are broad-based and modified for local context, texts and resource books/materials need to be focused on broad conceptual issues rather than the generic science coverage found in many grade-level science texts. Remember too that these units address some concepts not typically explored in depth (or breadth) in general science texts and therefore the standard grade level text may be too simplistic for students (and teachers). Some core textbook companies offer modules that teachers may choose from and others offer sets of materials that are concept focused. These might prove more appropriate if the content level is high enough and accurate. As is true with all types of curricular differentiation or problem-based learning, we recommend multiple resources be available, if not actually in the classroom, at least in the school.

Parents: Dealing with parental expectations was another concern that surfaced as participants tried to anticipate any issues or concerns facing their implementation of the units. One of the best suggestions offered by the groups was to bring the parents into the process early on, before actual start-up, and explain exactly what would happen and why and demonstrate how the science content would be covered in the activities. Having a file of PBL articles and research available for check-out in the library or on computer for parents (and other teachers) might also be useful. Finally, stress the point that this is also a good way to encourage girls to stay in math and science classes and careers, as the units provide models and experiences that demonstrate that girls/women can, in fact, "do" science and math.

State Standards or Reform Issues: Most state science standards or proficiency requirements acknowledge the need for and require attention to: problem solving skills, critical thinking skills, interdisciplinary problems, technology, and real-life applications and assessments. These units provide all of those elements and thus probably fit easily with many state and district requirements and reform issues. A review of standards and requirements would probably allow you to develop a check-off sheet showing where each element is embedded within the unit. This is great information to have available to share with parents, teachers, and administrators.

General Suggestions for Teachers:

1. Remember success is contagious. You are a terrific model and advocate! But collaboration and networking can help relieve some of the anxieties and stresses associated with trying to "go it alone." Set up a support team either at your own site or with another teacher/team implementing the units. Share your questions and successes. Do not re-invent the wheel!
2. Focus on how the units meet the needs of educational reform and change, high level critical thinking, interdisciplinarity, technology, relevant learning, authentic task assessments, and differentiation. Share that connection with other individuals, especially parents and administrators.
3. "Flexible" is the primary operating word. Always personalize the units to your own area and needs. Remember that the units will change each time you "teach" them and that it's expected, not an indication that something was done incorrectly!
4. You are not expected to provide all materials for the units. These units are intended to involve you as learner as well as facilitator. Delegate different resource acquisitions to different individuals, students, parents, and other educators.
5. Model curiosity, creativity and problem solving. How you deal with problems is a primary and immediate model for your students.

6. “Things take time” needs to be your personal operating motto.
7. Have fun and enjoy the experience! Both PBL and science are powerful organizers for instruction.

Monitoring Successful Reform

Just as implementation ideas for a new curriculum are important to share with teachers, it is equally important to ensure that a system for monitoring science classrooms exists that documents the nature of the science learning going on. It is recommended that the attached *Curriculum Reform Classroom Indicators* checklist be used by appropriate educational personnel to determine the extent of implementation occurring in classrooms. Principals, science coordinators, instructional leaders in schools all may employ the form to assess the success of science reform recommendations.

CURRICULUM REFORM CLASSROOM INDICATORS

Do our classrooms contain the following elements?

Yes **No**

____ ____ 1. Curriculum focuses on important concepts (e.g., systems, change, patterns, models).

____ ____ 2. Curriculum emphasizes the research process within an integrated framework (e.g., exploring a topic, planning how to study it and carrying out a study, judging results, and reporting).

____ ____ 3. Curriculum focuses on substantive content.

____ ____ 4. Instruction is inquiry-oriented, using strategies like problem-based learning and higher level questioning.

____ ____ 5. Instruction is activity-based, engaging students in the doing aspect of learning.

____ ____ 6. Assessment of learning includes performance-based approaches such as use of real-world problems for students to demonstrate understanding and transfer of key ideas and processes.

____ ____ 7. Assessment of learning includes a portfolio of student work including individual logs, reports, and other work.

____ ____ 8. Students engage in planning and carrying out original research. *(Teachers instruct students in experimental design.)*

____ ____ 9. Students actively discuss real-world problems and issues in relationship to societal implications. *(Teachers present scientific questions in classroom discussion and activities.)*

____ ____ 10. Students demonstrate thinking processes necessary for doing work in a given discipline (e.g., inference, deductive reasoning, evaluation of arguments). *(Teachers ask higher level thinking questions in classroom discussion and activities.)*

____ ____ 11. The curriculum materials used are appropriate for different ability levels and employ various approaches to learning.

____ ____ 12. The curriculum materials promote student engagement in learning.

____ ____ 13. Classroom instruction incorporates appropriate technology as a tool in learning.

____ ____ 14. Classroom instruction attends to individual differences in rate of learning as evidenced by small group or individually differentiated work.

Part VI

SCIENCE RESOURCES FOR TEACHERS AND PARENTS

Science Resources for Teachers and Parents

This section is intended to help parents and educators locate resources. It focuses on guides and sources that point the way to current science information and opportunities. In a few instances, it includes specific titles that particularly support the implementation of the William and Mary problem-based science curriculum.

Libraries

Public libraries provide a natural, comprehensive resource for inquisitive minds. Students and teachers should remember that the entire library is there to serve their needs. The Children's Services section has introductory books with clear explanations and illustrations for learners of all ages. Reference Services in the main section of the library offers guidance in exploring passionate interests and unknown subjects for both children and adults. The library staff in both the children's area and the reference area can assist in going beyond the library walls by providing assistance in using the Internet and electronic databases and by providing information about other area resources.

Academic libraries, especially those at public colleges and universities, generally permit use of their resources on site. Specialized reference materials and databases can be used by anyone at the library. Many academic libraries offer local or state residents a library card for a small annual fee.

Special libraries serve the needs of a specific group. For instance, corporations, museums and historical agencies, zoos, hospitals, and governments all have libraries with specialized research collections. The collections are frequently available for public use within the library walls. In fact, agencies with an education mission such as museums and governments often provide tailored, consultant reference service and unique resources for the student or adult researcher.

American Library Directory 1996–97. (49th ed.) 2 vols. New Providence, NJ: R.R. Bowker.

Arranged geographically, this directory lists all types of libraries. For each library, the entry includes name, address, phone number, and a description of holdings, special collections, and e-mail addresses. This directory is particularly useful for finding nearby libraries that specialize in a particular research interest or that specialize in area concerns.

Museums, Zoos, and Aquariums

Museums, zoos, and aquariums teach and entertain through fascinating displays and exhibits. In many science museums, such as San Francisco's Exploratorium, the exhibits are meant to be touched, manipulated, and explored. The displays, however, are only one function of museums, zoos and aquariums. The primary mission of many of the institutions is research and extending knowledge. Therefore, they offer extensive resources that go beyond the exhibits such as the employment of resident experts, publications, special programs, and volunteer or mentorship opportunities. Finding a museum that supports a special interest and then getting involved with the staff and programs offers unique opportunities for exploring a subject in-depth and for experiencing the excitement and the rigors of its research.

The Official Museum Directory, 1996. 2 vols. New Providence, NJ: R.R. Bowker.

Arranged geographically, this directory includes information about personnel, governing authority, collections and research fields, activities, publication hours, admission fees, and memberships. It is indexed by categories. Some of the categories under science include aquariums, marine museums and oceanariums, archaeology museums and archaeology sites, natural history and natural science museums, planetariums, observatories and astronomy museums, science museums and centers, and zoos. This directory is especially useful for planning trips.

Books

The books included here are not intended to provide a comprehensive list but to offer examples of helpful resources for parents and teachers in nurturing student interest in science.

Cothron, J.H., Giese, R.N., & Rezba, R.J. (1996). *Students and research: Practical strategies for science classrooms and competitions* (2nd ed.). Dubuque, IA: Kendall/Hunt Publishing Company.

Students and Research provides teachers with strategies for helping students from elementary grades to college levels develop research skills. It includes techniques for helping students design experiments, collect and analyze data, and write reports. Ideas for preparing for competitive events conclude the manual.

Cothron, J.H. Giese, R.N., & Rezba, R.J. (1996). *Science experiments and projects for students.* Dubuque, IA: Kendall/Hunt Publishing Company.

This manual is the student version of *Students and Research*. It guides students through each step of the research process.

Farrow, S. (1996). *The really useful science book: A framework of knowledge for primary teachers*. Washington, DC: Falmer.

Intended to support an understanding of the science content of the National Curriculum in Great Britain, this resource provides lucid and in-depth coverage of science content for teachers at the elementary level.

Leshin, C.B. (1995). *Internet adventures: Step-by-step guide for finding and using educational resources*. Paradise Valley, AZ: Xplora Publishing.

This guide is an example of the ever increasing number of resources for exploring the Internet. It provides both an explanation of the various aspects of the Internet and specific directions for finding information.

Saul, W., & Newman, A.R. (1986). *Science fare: An illustrated guide and catalog of toys, books, and activities for kids*. NY: Harper & Row.

Although some of the specifics in this book are somewhat dated, it is an invaluable resource, listing a wide variety of products and activities for young people. It also has excellent advice on choosing and using appropriate activities that appeal to a child's individual interests.

Periodicals

Appraisal reviews science books for young people. Each book is reviewed by both a scientist and a librarian who may have different perspectives as to the book's appeal or content. Address for subscription: Boston University School of Education, Children's Science Book Review Committee, 605 Commonwealth Avenue, Boston, MA 02215.

The New York Times publishes the "Science Times" as a special section of the paper every Tuesday. The coverage is timely, broad-ranging, interesting, and accurate. The articles are accessible to avid middle school readers and provide ideas for further investigation and reading. Address for subscription: New York Times, 229 W. 43rd Street, New York, NY 10036.

Scientific American includes in-depth articles that range from "The Origin of Horseback Riding" to "Quantum Cosmology and the Creation of the Universe," profiles of people in the science arena, a section of science issues called "Science and the Citizen," news of science and business, essays, science history, mathematical and scientific recreations, and book reviews. Each year the book review section in the December issue reviews books for young people and highlights a selection of the most exciting books published that year. Address for subscription: *Scientific American, Inc.,* 415 Madison Avenue, New York, NY 10017.

The Skeptical Inquirer reviews claims of paranormal phenomena such as astrology, ghosts, and Atlantis in a scientific manner, giving a reasoned treatment of the evidence for and against the claims. It is published by the Committee for the Scientific Investigation of the Claims of the Paranormal. Address for subscription: *Skeptical Inquirer,* Box 229, Buffalo, NY 14215-0229.

Bibliographies and Directories

Educational opportunity guide: A directory of programs for the gifted (1996). Durham, NC: Duke University Talent Identification Program.

Published annually, this directory lists educational programs for academically talented students of all ages. It includes information about programs in the United States and international programs, regional talent searches, state directors of gifted education, state and national associations for the gifted, and academic competitions. Subject indexes provide access to programs such as governor's summer schools, laboratory/internship programs, wilderness adventure/camp programs, and intense computer science institutes and camps.

National Science Resources Center. (1996). *Resources for teaching elementary school science* (1996). Washington, DC: National Academy Press.

In addition to describing hands-on, inquiry-based science curriculum materials, this guide highlights books on teaching science, science book lists and resource guides, periodicals, ancillary resources such as museums and other places to visit organized by state, professional associations and United States government organizations. A list of publishers and suppliers provides ordering information for materials and science apparatus. The directory offers a wealth of information to families and educators. A guide to resources for teaching middle school science is in preparation.

Once upon a time: Connecting young people's literature to Great Explorations in Math and Science (1993). Berkeley, CA: Lawrence Hall of Science, University of California, Berkeley.

This annotated bibliography of children's and young adult literature is designed to support the GEMS (Great Explorations in Math and Science) curriculum. It offers literature connections for each GEMS guide; for math strands: algebra, functions, geometry, logic, measurement, number pattern, probability and statistics; and for the ten major themes in science: diversity and unity, energy, evolution, matter, models and simulations, patterns of change, scale, stability, structure, systems and interactions. Periodic revisions to the guide are planned, and the *GEMS Newsletter* provides new titles on a regular basis.